# Service From the Heart

*Renewing the Ancient Path of Biblical Prayer and Service*

# Service From the Heart

*Renewing the Ancient Path of Biblical Prayer and Service*

First Edition

Oklahoma B'nai Noah Society

Rose, Oklahoma USA

© 1996-2007 Oklahoma B'nai Noah Society. All Rights Reserved. Except as permitted under the U.S. Copyright Act of 1976, no part of this book may be reproduced or distributed in any form without written permission from the publisher.

Published by OKBNS PRESS an imprint of Oklahoma B'nai Noah Society, 57527 S. 550 Rd., Rose, Oklahoma U.S.A. 74364
www.okbns.org

Copies in quantities of 25 or more are available directly from the publisher. Please email okbnspress@okbns.org.

Contributing Editors:

    Rabbi Michael Katz
    Rabbi Yechiel Sitzman
    Pam Rogers
    Larry Rogers
    Nancy January

Reviewed, Corrected and/or Approved by:

    Rabbi Yirmeyahu Bindman
    Rabbi Michael Katz
    Rabbi Yoel Schwartz
    Rabbi Yechiel Sitzman

Cover art by Larry Rogers
Cover design by Pam Rogers
Layout design and electronic files by Nancy January

First Edition October 2007

Paperback ISBN: 978-0-6151-6402-1

Hardcover ISBN: 978-0-6151-6578-3

Library of Congress Control Number: 2007937555

בס"ד

הנה הובאה לפני כמה רבנים הסידור שערכו כמה אנשים מבני נח וגם מבני ישראל ותמצא שסידור זה יכול לשמש כאוצר תפילות לכל מי שמבקש להתפלל אל ה'. הן לומר על פי סדר התפילות שבו והן לומר תפילות כפי נטיית לבו.

לכן ידינו לחזק את המוצאים לאור כי דבר גדול ונזקד הוא הסידור הזה, ומברכים את כל מי שיתן ידו להדפיס אותו.

### Approbation of Siddur

This siddur for Bnei Noah was brought for a critical evaluation before a number of rabbis who are involved in guiding Bnei Noah. This siddur was developed by a number of Bnei Noah and Jews. It provides a collection of texts that will be useful to those who wish to pray to G-d. This is good both for those who will want to utilize the entire text and those who will prefer to pick and choose according to the inclination of their heart.

Therefore we wish to encourage its producers because this siddur is an important work and we bless any one who will help publish it.

Rabbi Yoel Schwartz, Chief rabbi of a special Beit Din for Bnei Noah.

Rabbi Yechiel Sitzman.

# Contents

*Foreword* ..................................................................................... *i*

*About This Book* ........................................................................ *v*

*Purpose* ...................................................................................... *xi*

*Introduction to Noahide Prayers* ............................................ *xv*

*A Few Notes on Praying and Prayer* ...................................... *xix*

*Early Morning Blessings* ........................................................... *1*

    **Upon Awakening before Getting out of Bed** ............................. 1

    **After Leaving the Bathroom** ....................................................... 1

    **After getting Dressed for the Day** ............................................. 2

*Morning Service* ....................................................................... *11*

    **Shema** .......................................................................................... 11

    **Washing of the Hands** ............................................................... 12

    **Putting on the Prayer Garment** ................................................ 15

        The Fifth Psalm .................................................................... 18

        The Eighty-Sixth Psalm ....................................................... 20

## *Offerings* .................................................................. 29

### The Teachings of the Sages on Sacrifices and Prayer ........... 29

### The Offering ........................................................................ 34

### The Tradition of Job .......................................................... 38

#### The Hundred and Forty-Fifth Psalm .................................... 39
#### The Hundred and Forty-Sixth Psalm .................................... 42
#### The Hundred and Forty-Seventh Psalm ................................ 44
#### The Hundred and Forty-Eighth Psalm .................................. 46
#### The Hundred and Forty-Ninth Psalm ................................... 48
#### The Hundred and Fiftieth Psalm .......................................... 50

### Benediction ....................................................................... 54

### Shema ................................................................................ 58

## *Communal Prayers* ........................................................ 65

### Invitation to Worship ........................................................ 65

#### The Hundredth Psalm ........................................................... 65

### Prayer ................................................................................ 66

### GOD's Covenant ................................................................ 66

### GOD's Might .................................................................... 68

### GOD's Holiness ................................................................ 69

### Knowledge ........................................................................ 69

Repentance .......................................................................................... 70

Forgiveness ........................................................................................ 71

Redemption ....................................................................................... 71

Healing .............................................................................................. 71

Prosperity .......................................................................................... 72

For Times and Places Where There is a Natural Dry Season (not a drought) .............................................................................................. 72

For Times and Places When Rain is Needed ................................... 73

For All Seasons ................................................................................. 74

Ingathering of the Israelites ............................................................. 74

Justice ................................................................................................ 75

Against the Enemies of Israel .......................................................... 75

For the Righteous .............................................................................. 76

The Rebuilding of Jerusalem ........................................................... 77

Kingdom of David ............................................................................. 78

Response to Prayer ........................................................................... 78

Restoration of the Temple Service .................................................. 80

On the New Moon .............................................................................. 81

Thanksgiving ..................................................................................... 82

Peace .................................................................................................. 92

**Prayer for Parents** ............................................................... 93

**Prayer for Children** ............................................................... 94

**Prayer of Sustenance** ............................................................ 94

**Concluding Prayer** ................................................................ 96

**Personal or National Distress** .............................................. 98

    The Twentieth Psalm ............................................................. 98

**For the Welfare of Israel** .................................................... 100

    The Eighty-Third Psalm ....................................................... 100

**Concluding Psalm** ............................................................... 102

    The Sixty-Seventh Psalm .................................................... 102

## *Evening Reflections* ......................................................... *109*

**Meditations** ........................................................................... 109

**Bedtime Prayer** ..................................................................... 109

**Shema** ................................................................................... 111

## *Remembering the Seventh Day* ...................................... *119*

**Lighting the Candles** ........................................................... 119

    Psalm 1 .................................................................................. 121

**Blessing of the Children** ..................................................... 125

**Blessing of the Wine** ........................................................... 125

**Washing of the Hands** ......................................................... 126

  Blessing of the Bread ...................................................................... 127

  During the Meal .............................................................................. 128

  After the Meal ................................................................................. 128

    Psalm 92 ..................................................................................... 128

  Blessing after the Meal .................................................................... 131

*Seventh Day Noon Meal* ...................................................... *137*

  Blessing of the Wine ....................................................................... 137

  Washing of the Hands .................................................................... 138

  Blessing of the Bread ...................................................................... 139

*Seventh Day Evening Meal* .................................................. *143*

  Blessing of the Wine ....................................................................... 143

  Washing of the Hands .................................................................... 144

  Blessing of the Bread ...................................................................... 145

  Blessing after the Meal .................................................................... 145

*Havdalah* ............................................................................... *151*

  At the Close of the Seventh Day, after Sundown ........................ 151

  Blessing of the Wine ....................................................................... 152

  Sweet Smelling Spices .................................................................... 152

  For the Flames ................................................................................ 152

## Songs ... 159

### Hine Ma Tov (How Good and Pleasant it is) ... 159

### David Melekh Yisrael (David King of Israel) ... 159

### Haveinu Shalom Aleikhem (We Bring You Peace) ... 159

### Adon Olam (Master of the Universe) ... 160

## Additional Prayers and Blessings ... 165

### Blessings for Torah Study ... 165

Before study ... 165

After study ... 165

### Maimonides 13 Principles of Faith ... 166

### Morning Prayer ... 168

### Naming a Child ... 169

### Blessing a Child ... 170

### Prayers for Places of Idolatry ... 171

### Prayer for Places Where Idolatry has been Uprooted: ... 171

### Blessing Before or After a Meal ... 172

### Various Blessings for Food ... 172

Wine ... 172

Bread ... 172

For mixtures of different kinds of food in one meal ... 173

- Grain ........................................................................................... 173
- Tree grown fruit ........................................................................ 173
- Earth grown fruit or vegetables ................................................ 173

### Blessings for Various Events ................................................. 173

- When witnessing shooting stars, storms, thunderclaps, lightning and earthquakes: ........................................................ 173
- For rain and for good tidings ................................................... 174
- For bad tidings or news of a death .......................................... 174
- When seeing a rainbow ............................................................ 174

### Prayer for Travelers ................................................................. 174

### Prayer of Remembrance ........................................................... 176

### On Passing ................................................................................ 178

## *Readings From the Psalms* ..................................................... 185

### The Daily Psalms – 30 day Reading ........................................ 185

### Psalms for Special Circumstances .......................................... 186

- Prayer of Thanksgiving ............................................................ 186
- Safety of Israel ......................................................................... 186
- Personal Safety ........................................................................ 186
- Illness ....................................................................................... 186
- Recovery from Illness .............................................................. 186
- The Seventh Day ...................................................................... 186

    On the Wedding Day ................................................................. 186

    Giving Birth ................................................................................ 186

    Repentance ................................................................................. 186

    Peace ........................................................................................... 186

    To Strengthen Belief .................................................................. 186

    For Guidance ............................................................................. 186

    Rosh Chodesh (New Moon) ...................................................... 186

    Gratitude .................................................................................... 186

    Help with Troubles .................................................................... 186

    Traveling .................................................................................... 186

    Happiness ................................................................................... 187

    Mourning .................................................................................... 187

## *Wedding Ceremony ................................................................ 191*

    **A Few Customs** ....................................................................... 191

    **The Wedding Ceremony** ........................................................ 193

    **The Exchange of Rings** .......................................................... 195

    **The Blessings** .......................................................................... 197

## *Funeral Service ....................................................................... 205*

    **Introduction** ............................................................................ 205

    **The Service** ............................................................................. 206

Psalm 23 ............................................................................................. 208

Psalm 16 ............................................................................................. 211

## *The Seven Noahide Laws Revealed in Genesis* ............................ 217

1. Idolatry .................................................................................... 217
2. Blasphemy ............................................................................... 218
3. Murder ..................................................................................... 219
4. Theft ......................................................................................... 220
5. Forbidden Sexual Relationships ........................................... 221
6. Eating the Limb of a Living Animal ..................................... 221
7. Establishing Courts of Justice ............................................... 222

## *Brief History of B'nai Noah* ............................................................ 223

## *Noahide Theology* ............................................................................. 229

The Oral Tradition for Jews and Gentiles ................................. 229

Before the Flood ............................................................................ 230

After the flood ............................................................................... 231

## *Noahide Commandments* ................................................................ 235

Introduction ................................................................................... 235

Foreword ......................................................................................... 237

Commandments Dealing With Matters Between Man and GOD ................ 244

Commandments Dealing with Personal Matters ..................... 267

Commandments Dealing with Matters Between Man and His Fellow .........283

*About Disposal of this Siddur* ..........................................................**297**

*Glossary* ..............................................................................................**299**

*More Information* ..............................................................................**309**

    Online Education..................................................................................309

    Books ....................................................................................................309

    Torah Study..........................................................................................309

    Seven Laws of Noah Studies................................................................309

    Further Reading...................................................................................310

# Foreword

By
Rabbi Michael Katz
Miami, Florida USA

---

The most basic principle of life is gratitude.

Obedience to Torah is our expression of love and gratitude for the One Who has given us this tremendous opportunity to deserve His bounty. How can one say that he loves GOD with all his heart, soul, and might if one ignores GOD's will and fails to obey His commandments?

A corollary of gratitude is the avoidance of taking anything that does not belong to us. The Talmud (Bavli Berachos 35a) poses a contradiction: one verse in the Tenach tells us that all of this world belongs to GOD (Psalm 24:1) while another verse tells us that the Heavens belong to GOD while the Earth was given to man (Psalm 115:16).

The Talmud resolves this apparent contradiction by stating that before one thanks GOD for His bounty, everything belongs to Him, and it would be theft to take it. After expressing thanks to GOD, the bounty is released, and we are permitted to enjoy it.

Simply put, GOD is telling us that we cannot have the fruit until we say, "Thank you."

But GOD is not only teaching us manners, He is commanding us to be grateful.

Prayer is not specifically commanded to B'nai No'ach but that is only because it is the most obvious requirement of man. Certainly we can look at the episode of Abraham and Avimelech (Genesis 20) to see that prayer is both for Abraham and his descendants as well as for everyone else. In his vision, Avimelech is told by GOD to return Sarah to Abraham and then Abraham will pray for the healing of Avimelech and his household.

We could apply the lesson taught in the passage from Talmud Berachos, quoted above. Although this passage from the Talmud is being addressed to Jews, I do not see why it cannot be extended to include all of mankind. If it is wrong to enjoy the bounty provided by GOD without acknowledging His goodness, the obligation to express gratitude should apply to all. B'nai No'ach are not bound by the formulae created by the Sages for Jews, but they can find their own manner in which to express their thanks. It need not even be expressed verbally; thinking grateful thoughts while enjoying a tasty snack would be adequate for B'nai No'ach.

But, ultimately, none of that is necessary. Prayer is required of all mankind simply because to not pray to GOD is to insult Him. Not praying denies that GOD is the source of all that is good and has the power to provide all of our needs.

What form should prayer take? Here B'nai No'ach are given permission to give full expression to the depths of their gratitude. Let them give wings to their thoughts of love and reverence and find the words that most speak to their souls.

It is, however, a sign of the humility of the B'nai No'ach in our generation, that they are reluctant to compose their own prayers and, instead, they wish to turn to the traditional prayers composed by the Sages of old for the Jewish communities. This they can do with the proviso that they are careful not to utter any untruths. Thus, they must be careful not to imply that they are commanded to do activities that only Jews are commanded to do. They must be careful not to refer to the Patriarchs as their fathers since, in most cases, they are probably not.

The editors of this useful prayer book, a siddur for B'nai No'ach ("siddur" means "order" and refers to the orderly manner in which prayers are laid out) are to be commended for providing this means for B'nai No'ach to express their gratitude to God. Let this not be the final product but rather the foundation on which others will build and offer their own prayers that might speak better to their unique experiences.

My blessings to all who find comfort and regeneration in the words contained within this volume. May you continue to grow in your worship of the One True God of Israel and may the words of Genesis 12:3 be fulfilled in you and in your descendants.

# About This Book

This project began in 1996 due to the request of many Observant Noahides who wanted to know how to pray to their Creator in a proper way. In the beginning, we put prayers together in a very Jewish way, which the Rabbis were quick to correct. They explained that we could adapt some of the prayers from Jewish sources as long as we made them truthful for Noahides, as not all prayers are appropriate for non-Jews.

This prayer book could not have been accomplished if it hadn't been for the dedicated patience of the Rabbis and many Observant Noahides who painstakingly researched, submitted, reviewed, and gave us feed back on each prayer.

Some of the prayers were written by Rabbi Michael Katz and Rabbi Yirmeyahu Bindman and are included here with their permission. Others were written and/or re-written and organized by Observant Noahides from around the globe.

Much of the order of our communal prayers was researched and submitted by Koh Gee Tek Francis.

Unfortunately, through the years there have been many, many computer crashes and information has been lost.

The Scriptural text is from the 1611 King James Version (KJV) found at ebible.org, which is the only public domain English translation we had free access to. We did, however, replace the "Thees" and "Thous" and other archaic words and syntax with more modern terms and sentence structures to improve readability. For consistency we've used the KJV system of numbering chapters and verses. Readers using a translation from a Jewish publishing house will notice a few differences in the numbering system. So in some instances the references will be off a verse or so.

Because the Hebrew scriptural texts only provide us with the consonants of GOD's name—omitting the vowels—the correct pronunciation of GOD's name is unknown. So wherever the Divine Name would otherwise be pronounced, we have followed the centuries-long tradition of using "the LORD," "LORD," or "GOD." The words "Lord" and "God" are used when referring to titles or rank, such as "Lord of …" or "God of …," and are not referring to the Divine Name itself.

Words in *italics*, except those which are part of scripture quotations, are explanations or instructions and are not intended to be read aloud, although one may certainly choose to do so if he/she wishes.

We have also included lines on the "notes" pages in the hope that it will encourage readers to actually write on these pages and make this book truly individualized for them.

We have made every effort to avoid copyright infringement. However, as with any work compiled from multiple sources, something may have been missed. We will certainly make the appropriate correction if an oversight is brought to our attention.

No person involved in this eleven-year work receives any personal compensation from the sale of this book. All proceeds help with future projects, build the Noahide Community world wide, provide charity funds, and provide a service fund for prison outreach.

We would like to acknowledge all of those who have helped on this project through the years, if we have forgotten anyone, please let us know and we will correct the error in future editions.

The list of those whom we can't thank enough:

GOD, The Creator of all things!
Rabbi Yirmeyahu Bindman (Israel)
Rabbi Tuvia Bolton (Israel)
Rabbi Yehoshua Friedman (Israel)
Rabbi Yeshayahu Hollander (Israel)
Rabbi Michael Katz (United States)
Rabbi Yoel Schwartz (Israel)

Rabbi Shmuel Silinsky (Israel)
Rabbi Yechiel Sitzman (Israel)
Chris Bell (United States)
Jackie Damron (United States)
Ephraim Eliyahu, VirtualYeshiva.com (United States)
Aryeh Gallin, Root and Branch (Israel)
Reuven Ginat (Israel)
Donnie January, Oklahoma B'nai Noah Society (United States)
Nancy January, Oklahoma B'nai Noah Society (United States)
Koh Gee Tek Francis (Singapore)
Terry Lanham, Chavurath Bnei Noach (United States)
Yaacov Levi (United States)
Frances Makarova, Moderated Noahides Discussion List (Australia)
Larry Rogers, Oklahoma B'nai Noah Society (United States)
Pam Rogers, Oklahoma B'nai Noah Society (United States)
Richard Rose (United States)
Jack Saunders (United States)
Andrea Woodward (United States)

We would also like to thank:

Aish.com for permission to use material from their website.

The *B'nai Noah Quarterly* for allowing us to use portions of their article "Sabbath Celebration" published in 2000 in our publication *Shabbat: a Celebration for the Non-Jew* © 2002

Oklahoma B'nai Noah Society which is reprinted in full here beginning with the "Remembering the Seventh Day" section and ending with the "Havdalah" section.

Frances Makarova for allowing us to reprint "The Seven Laws Revealed in Genesis" from www.geocities.com/rachav.

Rabbi Pliskin for permission to use material from *Gateway to Self-Knowledge*.

Rabbi Yoel Schwartz for permission to reprint the English translation of "Noahide Commandments" from his book *Atem Adi*.

# Purpose

This prayer book is submitted for voluntary use by B'nai Noah first and foremost because there are many B'nai Noah who express concern that they do not know the proper way to pray to their Creator. For them, this book can be a guide to the proper approach to GOD through prayer—not an absolute requirement, but a tool to use as they determine the need. At the end of each section we have included pages for individuals to include additional information and personal notes.

Secondly, this book is submitted for B'nai Noah who have asked for communal prayers.

Having a liturgical tradition fills a spiritual need in man that cannot be filled any other way, for it brings opposing forces into unity without destroying the unique characteristics of those forces—and does so on many levels simultaneously.

On the most obvious level, it provides beautiful and eloquent words of faith, devotion, and understanding for those who find it difficult to find words of their own to express the stirrings in their hearts. In doing so, it frees them from their struggle with vocabulary so that they may concentrate on their worship and achieve a deeper spiritual experience.

Those whose command of language is eloquent and fluent, on the other hand, are freed from the need to be always creating new expressions of their faith, devotion, and understanding, so that the old can become familiar, sustaining friends, ready to be used when the heart is too filled with emotion to sort the words out.

A common liturgy brings the voices of the eloquent and the ineloquent together in one voice, erasing the differences between them as they share their words in worship, thus bringing them into unity. Once joined in verbal unity, they enter into a unity of identity.

In praying together, we agree in word and spirit, publicly announcing our agreement through voiced unity. We become one people—a whole made up of individuals. No voice stands before the others, for each voice is absorbed by the next, adding its own life, then sending it forth to be added to another until each is a part of all, inseparable and indistinguishable from the others. The individual, thus bonded to other worshipers, is supported and freed from the pressures and vexations that are unique to him—freed to rest in the awareness that no man stands alone against the world so long as he can enter in the united identity of B'nai Noah.

United identity achieved through common liturgy is not limited to the time, space, or people sharing its immediate experience; it bonds each worshipper to every other who has stood, or will stand, before GOD proclaiming "Hear, O Israel, the LORD our God, the

LORD is One," renewing our covenant again on an individual basis. Even though each worshipper brings a different knowledge of time, space, and experience to collective worship, they become united in voice, in identity, in covenantal relationship with GOD through the simple act of speaking words of worship together.

In time, the B'nai Noah community will develop other prayer books. May this volume be but the beginning….

# Introduction to Noahide Prayers

Excerpted from "Noahide Commandments"
(Rabbi Yoel Schwartz, *Atem Adai*)
Translated by Yitzhak A. Oked Sechter
Reviewed and corrected by Rabbi Yechiel Sitzman
in consultation with Rabbi Yoel Schwartz

---

The basis of all commandments is the belief that GOD, Who is the creator of all things, and capable of doing everything, has commanded us to fulfill them. Habakkuk summed it up by stating that a righteous person shall live through his belief. Also in Chapter 9:23 of Jeremiah it is stated: "But let he who glories, glory in this, that he understands and knows Me, that I am the LORD who exercises loving kindness, judgment and righteousness in the world: for it is these things that I desire, says the LORD."

The Gaon, Rabbi Shmuel Ben Hafni, stated that the important commandment for the people of other nations is the belief that the LORD our God is the Creator and director of the world, that He is actively involved in the lives of every person, and that He is One.

The Rambam writing to Rav Hasdai stated: "Quoting from our sages, the righteous people from other nations have a place in the world to come, if they have acquired what they should learn about the Creator."

In the category of the belief in the one true God, the seven commandments to the children of Noah include the prohibitions against worshiping other gods and against blasphemy (which includes professing atheism). There are, of course, many commandments connected with the belief in the one true God. They include:

A. Loving GOD
B. **Praying to Him** [bold is Editor's emphasis]
C. Thanking Him for His generosity
D. Trusting Him
E. Honoring Him
F. Sanctifying His Holy Name
G. Prohibiting the desecration of His Holy Name
H. Moving away from those who do not believe in Him such as atheists, infidels and impious people
I. Having a direct relationship with Him, not through any intermediaries. This is why it is forbidden to pray among others to any angels or to the dead or to any person past, present or future!

A. Loving GOD: Inasmuch as the Israelites were commanded not only to love GOD, but that they should also teach all mankind to love GOD, we see that all people are supposed to love Him. One of the first to do so was Abraham the Patriarch (Sifri Vetchanan), and in the Sefer Mitzvot it says, "This mitzvah [loving GOD] includes that we should call every human being to believe in Him and worship only

Him... See to it that you make Him beloved to your fellow men just as your forefather Abraham did."

B. **Praying to GOD**: Noah was punished for not praying so that his fellow men might be saved from the flood. According to the sages (Zohar Leviticus p15b), this is the reason that the flood is named after Noah. However, the destruction of Sodom is another case. This event is not named after Abraham because he did pray to save the people of Sodom before it was destroyed. One type of prayer is a request by a human being to GOD. There is also a thanksgiving prayer that is an important obligation from a person for all the things for which he is thankful such as: his occupation that gives him a livelihood, health, family, etc. and especially if something good has occurred to him personally. This brings us to thanksgiving.

C. Thanking GOD for His generosity: Again the best example is from Abraham. In the Gemara Sota 10, Abraham in Beersheva would invite people to eat and drink with him. At the end of the meal he would request from them that they should bless and thank GOD for His generosity.

*For a complete copy of Rabbi Yoel Schwartz's "Noahide Commandments" please see page 235.*

REMINDER: This prayer book is intended to be a guide for those who wish to utilize it. It should be clearly understood that we do not in any way attempt or intend to say that Non-Jews are commanded to use these particular prayers.

# A Few Notes on Praying and Prayer

By
Pam Rogers

---

Prayers should always be directed to GOD, Creator of the Universe, without Whom all things would cease to exist, and to Him alone, and not to an intermediary.

We should never say what is not in our heart; GOD doesn't want us to merely read words on a page; He wants us to draw close to Him.

As Rabbi Schwartz points out "There are several types of prayers: requests, recognition of GOD's grandeur, thanksgiving to Him for good things that He has done for a person, and strengthening one's faith." There are also emergencies, health issues, etc. Of course, GOD knows all of these things, but if we don't talk to Him and include Him in our daily existence, then we are in fact denying His existence and our need for Him as the Creator and Orchestrater of our lives.

He wants us to talk to Him and tell Him about everything, not because He needs it, but because we do. We need to remember that GOD is in control. We need to receive comfort from knowing that He is orchestrating all that exists. We need to remember that He is in charge, and that we should choose life by following after His guidance. Without His help and guidance, we are in essence grappling through the dark and are unable to reach our true and full potential.

Another important thing to remember is that we have free choice. That means that GOD will not force Himself on us. We must freely choose to serve Him. In part that is what our prayers do. They show our choice to accept GOD's help and guidance in our lives.

On another note, while we are praying, we should remember that we are addressing GOD, Creator of the Universe and that we should show Him more respect than we would a President or earthly king. It is the King of all kings whom we are, in fact, talking to.

We would never, for instance, greet an earthly dignitary without being properly clothed. Or greet a king in the bathroom where we take care of our bodily needs. So we should not address our GOD in such a manner either.

**About bowing**

A friend of mine reminded me that when Jews bow they also bend their knees. So I looked into the Tanakh and found this scripture:

Isaiah 45:20-24

Assemble yourselves and come; draw near together, you *that are* escaped of the nations: they have no knowledge that set up the wood of their graven image, and pray unto a god *that* cannot save.

Tell you, and bring *them* near; yes, let them take counsel together: Who has declared this from ancient time? *Who* has told it from that time? H*a*ve not I the LORD? And *there is* no God else beside Me; a just God and a Savior; *there is* none beside Me.

Look unto Me, and be you saved, all the ends of the earth: for I *am* GOD, and *there is* none else. I have sworn by Myself, the word is gone out of My mouth *in* righteousness, and shall not return, That unto Me every knee shall bow, every tongue shall swear.

Surely, shall *one* say, in the LORD have I righteousness and strength: *even* to Him shall *men* come; and all that are incensed against Him shall be ashamed.

So we would like to suggest that when a bow or bowing is suggested in the text that in fulfillment of this scripture we bend the knees, bow forward at the waist, bow at the head then rise up and straighten the legs.

*Early Morning*

*Blessings*

*Blessed are You, LORD our God, King of the Universe, Who removes sleep from my eyes and slumber from my eyelids.*

# *Early Morning Blessings*

## Upon Awakening before Getting out of Bed

I thank You, O Living and Eternal King, for restoring my soul to me with compassion; great is Your faithfulness.

## After Leaving the Bathroom

Blessed are You, LORD our God, King of the Universe, Who has formed man in wisdom and created in him many orifices and hollow passages. It is revealed and known before Your Glorious Throne, that should any one of those be opened or any one of those be closed inappropriately, it would be impossible for man to survive or stand before You.

Blessed are You, LORD, Who heals all flesh and perform wonders.

## After getting Dressed for the Day

O my God, the soul which You placed within me is pure. You created it, You formed it, You breathed it into me, and You preserve it within me. You will one day take it from me, but will restore it to me in the hereafter. So long as the soul is within me, I will give thanks to You, LORD my God, Master of all works, Lord of all souls!

Blessed are You, LORD, Who restores the souls to the dead.

Blessed are You, LORD our God, King of the Universe, Who has given the heart intelligence to distinguish between day and night.

Blessed are You, LORD our God, King of the Universe, Who has ordained the Covenant of the Rainbow.

Blessed are You, LORD our God, King of the Universe, Who has allowed me freedom to serve You.

Blessed are You, LORD our God, King of the Universe, Who gives sight to the blind.

Blessed are You, LORD our God, King of the Universe, Who clothes the naked.

Blessed are You, LORD our God, King of the Universe, Who sets the captive free.

Blessed are You, LORD our God, King of the Universe, Who straightens the bent.

Blessed are You, LORD our God, King of the Universe, Who spreads out the earth above the waters.

Blessed are You, LORD our God, King of the Universe, Who provides me with all my needs.

Blessed are You, LORD our God, King of the Universe, Who has made firm the steps of man.

Blessed are You, LORD our God, King of the Universe, Who gives strength to the weary.

Blessed are You, LORD our God, King of the Universe, Who removes sleep from my eyes and slumber from my eyelids.

Be praised, LORD, for the renewal of life.

My Master, I have sinned before You.

May it be Your will, LORD, my God, to grant me a good heart, a good portion, a good inclination, a good friend, a good name, a good eye, a good soul, a lowly disposition, and a humble spirit.

May Your Name never be profaned because of us, and may we never become an object of gossip among people.

May our lives not terminate in sudden destruction, or our hope turn to frustration. Do not cause us to be dependent on the gifts of mortals, and may our livelihood not depend on creatures of flesh and blood.

May our portion be in the study of Your Torah of the Seven Laws, together with those who heed Your will. Restore Your House, Your Temple, Your City, Your Shrine, speedily, in our time.

Heavenly Master, at the dawn of a new day, hear our voice. You are the Source of our strength. We commend the results of our labor into Your hands; may they be deemed worthy of Your approval. Grant us, O Divine Source of Strength, the power to toil patiently and to hope for Your blessing.

May this day and every day bring us nearer to You. Amen.

*Here ends the Early Morning Blessings.*

*Personal Notes*

*Service From the Heart*

*Early Morning Blessings*

*Service From the Heart*

# Morning Service

*But as for me, my prayer is unto You, O LORD, in an acceptable time: O GOD, in the multitude of Your mercy hear me, in the truth of Your salvation.*

*Psalm 69:13*

## *Morning Service*

The fear of the LORD is the beginning of wisdom; all who practice it have good sense. His praise endures forever.

May the Torah of the Seven Laws be my faith and Almighty GOD my help.

**Shema**

> *We, as Observant Noahides, no matter what our differences of culture from around the globe, share the same origins back to Adam. When we individually or collectively choose to do and accept the ways of GOD as defined by Torah, with Israel as our Teachers-Priests, we link our destiny to that of Israel. Therefore, it is appropriate to confirm our solidarity by saying the Shema along with Israel.*

Hear O Israel, the LORD our God, the LORD is One. (Deuteronomy 6:4)

> *The next paragraph is traditionally said in a whisper.*

Blessed be His Name Whose Glorious Kingdom is forever and ever!

And the LORD God commanded the man, saying, "Of every tree of the garden you may freely eat." (Genesis 2:16)

But flesh with the life thereof, *which is* the blood thereof, you shall not eat. (Genesis 9:4)

And these words, which I command you this day, shall be in your heart: And you shall teach them diligently unto your children, and shall talk of them when you sit in your house, and when you walk by the way, and when you lie down, and when you rise up. (Deuteronomy 6:6-7)

**Washing of the Hands**

*The only reason to ask a Ben Noah to wash his/her hands is out of respect for prayers and as a reminder that every person should have hands that are clean from wrong doing toward his fellow man. For these purposes any method of washing hands should suffice. (Rabbi Yoel Schwartz)*

**Suggested Meditation**

Psalm 24:3-5

Who shall ascend into the hill of the LORD? or who shall stand in His holy place?

He that hath clean hands, and a pure heart; who hath not lifted up his soul unto vanity, nor sworn deceitfully.

He shall receive the blessing from the LORD, and righteousness from the God of his salvation.

**Continue**

We will walk with the throng to the House of our God.

**If one prays in a synagogue add**

How goodly are your tents, O Jacob, Your dwelling places, O Israel! (Numbers 24:5)

## If one prays in the Temple area, bow and say

I will come *into* Your House in the multitude of Your mercy: *and* in awe of You will I worship toward Your Holy Temple. (Psalm 5:7)

## Rise and continue

My prayer *is* unto You, O LORD, *in* an acceptable time: O GOD, in the multitude of Your mercy hear me, in the truth of Your salvation. (Psalm 69:13)

For it is written, "O Heeder of prayer, unto You does all flesh come." (Psalm 65:3)

I am but a stranger in the midst of Your People. May my prayer that I offer in this place, be answered, for it is said in the prayer of King Solomon when he dedicated the First Temple,

> Also, a gentile who is not of Your People Israel, but will come from a distant land, for Your Name's sake – for they will hear of Your Great Name and Your strong hand and

Your outstretched arm – and will come and pray toward this Temple – may You hear from Heaven, the foundation of Your abode, and act according to all that the gentile calls out to You, so that all the peoples of the world may know Your Name, to fear You as Your People Israel do, and to know that Your Name is proclaimed upon this Temple that I have built. (Adapted from 1 Kings 8:41-43)

*Some choose to offer a bow of gratitude, then rise and say*

LORD, I have loved the habitation of Your house, and the place where Your honor dwells. (Psalm 26:8)

I will prostrate myself toward Your Holy Temple in awe of You. (Psalm 5:7)

*Some offer an obeisance of three bows here.*

## Putting on the Prayer Garment

*Some choose the tradition of putting on a special garment for prayer. It is suggested that the color schemes reflect the Covenant of the Rainbow. Whether it is in the form of a robe, scarf, or shawl, wear it in the spirit of reverence and humility and meditate on the following.*

What is man, that You are mindful of him? And the son of man, that You visit him?

For You have made him a little lower than the angels, and have crowned him with glory and honor. (Psalm 8:4-5)

The LORD *is* good to all: and his tender mercies *are* over all his works. (Psalm 145:9)

Give unto the LORD the glory due unto His Name; worship the LORD in the beauty of holiness. (Psalm 29:2)

O LORD our Lord, how excellent is Your name in all the earth! (Psalm 8:9)

How excellent *is* Your loving kindness, O GOD! Therefore the children of men put their trust under the shadow of Your wings. (Psalm 36:7)

O LORD my God, in You do I put my trust. (Psalm 7:1)

And GOD said, "This *is* the token of the covenant which I make between Me and you and every living creature that *is* with you, for perpetual generations." (Genesis 9:12)

I am the servant of the Holy One, blessed be He, before Whom and before Whose Glorious Torah (Teachings) I bow down at all times.

Not on man do I rely, nor do I lean on a created being, but only on the God of the Heavens, Who is the God of Truth, Whose Torah is Truth, Whose Prophets are Prophets of Truth, and Who abounds in doing goodness and truth.

In Him alone is my trust, and to His Holy and Glorious Name I utter praises.

**When service begins at dawn, this psalm is suggested**

## The Fifth Psalm

To the chief Musician upon Nehiloth, A Psalm of David.

Give ear to my words, O LORD, consider my meditation.

Hearken unto the voice of my cry, my King, and my God: for unto You will I pray.

My voice shall You hear in the morning, O LORD; in the morning will I direct *my prayer* unto You, and will look up.

For You *are* not a God that has pleasure in wickedness: neither shall evil dwell with You.

The foolish shall not stand in Your sight: You hate all workers of iniquity.

You shall destroy them that speak lies: the LORD will abhor the bloody and deceitful man.

But as for me, I will come *into* Your House in the multitude of Your mercy: *and* in Your fear will I worship toward Your Holy Temple.

Lead me, O LORD, in Your righteousness because of my enemies; make Your way straight before my face.

For *there is* no faithfulness in their mouth; their inward part *is* very wickedness; their throat *is* an open sepulcher; they flatter with their tongue.

Destroy You them, O GOD; let them fall by their own counsels; cast them out in the multitude of their transgressions; for they have rebelled against You.

But let all those that put their trust in You rejoice: let them ever shout for joy, because You defend them: let them also that love Your Name be joyful in You.

For You, LORD will bless the righteous; with favor will You compass him as *with* a shield.

**This Psalm is suggested for the rest of the morning**

**The Eighty-Sixth Psalm**

A Prayer of David.

Bow down Your ear, O LORD, hear me: for I *am* poor and needy.

Preserve my soul; for I *am* steadfast: O You my God, save Your servant that trusts in You.

Be merciful unto me, O LORD: for I cry unto You daily.

Rejoice the soul of Your servant: for unto You, O LORD, do I lift up my soul.

For You, LORD *are* good, and ready to forgive; and plenteous in mercy unto all them that call upon You.

Give ear, O LORD, unto my prayer; and attend to the voice of my supplications.

In the day of my trouble I will call upon You: for You will answer me.

Among the gods *there is* none like unto You, O LORD; neither *are there any works* like unto Your works.

All nations whom You have made shall come and worship before You, O LORD; and shall glorify Your name.

For You *are* great, and do wondrous things: You *are* God alone.

Teach me Your way, O LORD; I will walk in Your truth: unite my heart to fear Your Name.

I will praise You, O LORD my God, with all my heart: and I will glorify Your Name for evermore.

For great *is* Your mercy toward me: and You have delivered my soul from the lowest hell.

O GOD, the proud are risen against me, and the assemblies of violent *men* have sought after my soul; and have not set You before them.

But You, O LORD, *are* a God full of compassion, and gracious, longsuffering, and plenteous in mercy and truth.

O turn unto me, and have mercy upon me; give Your strength unto Your servant, and save the son of Your handmaid.

Show me a token for good; that they which hate me may see *it,* and be ashamed:

because You, LORD have helped me, and comforted me.

**Continue**

Enter into His gates with thanksgiving, *and* into His courts with praise: be thankful unto Him, *and* bless His Name.

For the LORD *is* good; His mercy *is* everlasting; and His truth *endures* to all generations. (Psalm 100:4-5)

*Here ends the Morning Service*

*Personal Notes*

*Morning Service*

*Service From the Heart*

# Offerings

*Let my prayer be set forth before You as incense; and the lifting up of my hands as the evening sacrifice.*

*Psalm 141:2*

# *Offerings*

## The Teachings of the Sages on Sacrifices and Prayer

There were seven laws given to the Children of Noah, the negative laws against idolatry, murder, blasphemy, theft, eating the limb from a living animal, improper sexual relationships, and the positive law to establish courts of justice. Non-Jews were not commanded to sacrifice, but are allowed to make sacrifices almost any place they want. They could not themselves sacrifice at the Temple but they could submit a sacrifice to be offered there on his behalf by the Jews even if he were an idolater. (Mishnah Torah, Hilkoth Maaseh Akorbanoth 3:2-3)

(Though Noahides are permitted to sacrifice almost any place they want, they may not sacrifice in any manner they want. Noahides must seek instruction from Jews as to the manner in which an animal is sacrificed. Since Jews no longer are familiar with animal sacrifice, such instruction is no longer available, rendering moot the possibility of animal sacrifice before the Messianic Age.) (Rabbi Michael Katz )

The sages teach us that after Adam was expelled, he repented of his sins by returning to the very place he was created and building an altar. It was upon this spot that the descendents of Adam would come to and offer their sacrifices. Adam was the first person to return through repentance to closeness with GOD. (Zohar 55a, 55b, pages 234-5)

After the flood, Noah rebuilt the altar that Adam had originally built but was destroyed during the flood. But because he had a wound from an incident that happened on the Ark, Noah was not fit to offer sacrifices, so the "Priesthood" then passed on to Shem who, while not the oldest of Noah's sons, was the foremost in wisdom and piety. So, it is Shem who actually performed the sacrificial offerings. (See Va Yikra Rabba 20:1, Tanchuma, Noah 9., Sanhedrin 69b, Bereshit Rabbah 26:3, Rashi on Genesis 5:2)

This same spot, where Noah built his altar, where Shem would come to offer sacrifices, and later Abraham, Isaac, and Jacob would also offer sacrifices is located on the temple mount, the same spot where the Temple of GOD stood and will one day stand again. (According to the tradition: Rambam: Hil. Beis HaBechirah)

The importance of these things is that the spot where the Temple stood, where Adam, Noah, Shem, Abraham, Isaac, and Jacob made their sacrifices is Jerusalem. (See Rabbi Kaplan's Anthology, Volume 2, *Eye of the Universe*). Further notice that the altars were all established before Jacob became Israel. (Genesis 35) (B'reishith Rabbah 14:6)

Even while in the wilderness, sacrifices were being offered in front of the Tabernacle on the Altar. Israel even offered specific sacrifices for the seventy nations during Succot. These sacrifices took place every day during the seven day period, starting first at thirteen bulls, and decreasing it by one each day until on the seventh day, seven bulls were sacrificed, for a total of seventy. (Succah 55b)

When the Temple was destroyed, and the diaspora began, and it was no longer possible to offer sacrifices in the appropriate manner according to Torah, the sacrifices became speaking the words aloud. The Tanakh lists several references for oral sacrifice (prayer) rather than blood or meal sacrifices: Isaiah 1:11-18, Proverbs 16:6, 21:3, Micah 6:7-8, Hosea 6:6. Before the Temple was built, King David states in Psalm 51:16-21, that GOD does not want blood sacrifices but a contrite heart is true sacrifice.

Isaiah 56:6-8 informs us that sacrifices will be reinstated in the days of the third Temple and that the offerings of the seventy nations will be accepted once again when His House becomes a House of Prayer (sacrifices) for all nations. (see also Zechariah 14:1-21)

Prayer is what brings us closer to a true relationship with GOD. It is not because GOD needs to hear it but for us to realize that our lives are not our own. We belong to GOD. It is He who gives life and mercy and wisdom. It is

He who creates for us the world and everything in it. Our prayers are how we communicate with Him.

Prayer may serve as a request for aid, for health, for the sake of others. It may be giving thanks for sustenance, an increase in prosperity or wisdom, or just for the sight of the rainbow in the sky. Prayer has many purposes and may be considered as a personal moment between Creator and creation.

Prayer may be spoken aloud or silently, but should be with the mouth and not just the thought. (Psalm 21:3, among others). It is not the words from this book that makes prayer effective, as it is only meant as a guide, but the heart and mind of the person saying the prayers.

The entire world is experiencing its own part of the exile from closeness to GOD and His redemption. One day, and may that day come soon, Isaiah's prophecy (Isaiah 11:9) will be fulfilled that the knowledge of GOD will once again fill the Earth, and the prophecy of Zephaniah 3:9, that the entire Earth will call to Him with one voice, and He will turn to them.

## The Offering

Let my prayer be set forth before You *as* incense; *and* the lifting up of my hands *as* the evening sacrifice. (Psalm 141:2)

And Noah built an altar unto the LORD; and took of every clean beast, and of every clean fowl, and offered burnt offerings on the altar.

And the LORD smelled a sweet savor; and the LORD said in His heart, "I will not again curse the ground any more for man's sake; for the imagery of man's heart *is* evil from his youth; neither will I again smite anymore everything living, as I have done. While the earth remains, seedtime and harvest, and cold and heat, and summer and winter, and day and night shall not cease." (Genesis 8:20-21)

And GOD blessed Noah and his sons, and said unto them, "Be fruitful and multiply and replenish the earth.

"And the fear of you and the dread of you shall be upon every beast of the earth, and upon every fowl of the air, *upon* all that moves upon earth, and upon all the fish of the sea; into your hand are they delivered.

"Every moving thing that lives shall be meat for you; even as the green herb have I given you all things.

"But flesh with the life thereof, *which is* the blood thereof, shall you not eat.

"And surely your blood of your lives I will require; at the hand of every beast will I require it, and at the hand of man; at the hand of every man's brother I will require the life of man.

"Whoso sheds man's blood, by man shall his blood be shed: for in the image of GOD made He man.

"And you, be you fruitful, and multiply; bring forth abundantly in the earth and multiply therein."

And GOD spoke unto Noah, and to his sons with him saying, "And I, behold, I establish My Covenant with you, and with your seed after you; and with every living creature that *is* with you, of the fowl, of the cattle, and with every beast of the field with you, of all that go out of the Ark, to every beast of the earth.

"And I will establish My Covenant with you, neither shall all flesh be cut off any more by the waters of a flood; neither shall there anymore be a flood to destroy the earth."

And GOD said, "This *is* the token of the covenant that I make between Me and you and every living creature that *is* with you, for perpetual generations: I do set My bow in the cloud, and it shall be for a token of a covenant between Me and the earth.

"And it shall come to pass, when I bring a cloud over the earth, that the bow shall be seen in the cloud: and I will remember My Covenant, which *is* between Me and you and every living creature of all flesh; and the waters shall no more become a flood to destroy all flesh.

"And the bow shall be in the cloud; and I will look upon it, that I may remember the everlasting covenant between GOD and every living creature of all flesh that *is* upon the earth."

And GOD said unto Noah, "This *is* the token of the covenant, that I have established between Me and all flesh that *is* upon the earth."

And the sons of Noah that went forth of the ark were Shem, Ham, and Japheth: and Ham is the father of Canaan.

These *are* the three sons of Noah: and of them was the whole earth overspread. (Genesis 9:1-19)

## The Tradition of Job

*Some choose to recite one Psalm as an offering for each of their children. Rabbi Yoel Schwartz says that "Reciting these every day may be too much, as Job only brought his sacrifices once a week. One is free to do so if he/she wishes."*

## The Hundred and Forty-Fifth Psalm

A psalm of praise by David

I will exalt You, my God, O King; and I will bless Your Name forever and ever.

Every day will I bless You; and I will praise Your Name forever and ever.

Great *is* the LORD and greatly to be praised; and His greatness *is* unsearchable.

One generation shall praise Your works to another, and shall declare Your mighty acts.

I will speak of the glorious honor of Your majesty, and of Your wondrous works.

And *men* shall speak of the might of Your terrible acts: and I will declare Your greatness.

They shall abundantly utter the memory of Your great goodness, and shall sing of Your righteousness.

The LORD *is* gracious, and full of compassion; slow to anger, and of great mercy.

The LORD *is* good to all: and His tender mercies *are* over all His works.

All Your works shall praise You, O LORD; and Your saints shall bless You.

They shall speak of the glory of Your Kingdom, and talk of Your power;

To make known to the sons of men His mighty acts, and the glorious majesty of His Kingdom.

Your Kingdom *is* an everlasting kingdom, and Your dominion *endures* throughout all generations.

The LORD upholds all that fall and raises up all *those that be* bowed down.

The eyes of all wait upon You; and You give them their meat in due season.

You open Your hand, and satisfy the desire of every living thing.

The LORD is righteous in all His ways and holy in all His works.

The LORD *is* nigh unto all them that call upon Him, to all that call upon Him in truth.

He will fulfill the desire of them that fear Him: He also will hear their cry, and will save them.

The LORD preserves all them that love Him: but all the wicked will He destroy.

My mouth shall speak the praise of the LORD: and let all flesh bless His Holy Name forever and ever.

## The Hundred and Forty-Sixth Psalm

Praise you the LORD. Praise the LORD, O my Soul.

While I live will I praise the LORD: I will sing praises unto to my God while I have any being.

Put not your trust in princes, *nor* in the son of man, in whom *there is* no help.

His breath goes forth, he returns to his earth; in that day his thoughts perish.

Happy *is he* that *has* the God of Jacob for his help, whose hope *is* in the LORD his God:

Who made heaven, and earth, the sea, and all that therein *is*:

Who keeps Truth for ever:

Who executes judgment for the oppressed:

Who gives food to the hungry.

The LORD releases the prisoners:

The LORD opens *the eyes of* the blind:

The LORD raises them that are bowed down:

The LORD loves the righteous:

The LORD preserves the strangers; He relieves the fatherless and widow: but the way of the wicked He turns upside down.

The LORD shall reign forever, *even* your God, O Zion, unto all generations. Praise you the LORD.

## The Hundred and Forty-Seventh Psalm

Praise you the LORD: for *it is* good to sing praises unto our God; for *it is* pleasant; *and* praise is comely.

The LORD does build up Jerusalem: He gathers together the outcasts of Israel.

He heals the broken in heart, and binds up their wounds.

He tells the number of the stars; He calls them all by *their* names.

Great *is* our Lord, and of great power: His understanding *is* infinite.

The LORD lifts up the meek: He casts the wicked down to the ground.

Sing unto the LORD with thanksgiving; sing praise upon the harp unto our God:

Who covers the heaven with clouds, Who prepares rain for the earth, Who makes grass to grow upon the mountains.

He gives to the beast his food, *and* to the young ravens which cry.

He delights not in the strength of the horse: He takes not pleasure in the legs of a man.

The LORD takes pleasure in them that fear Him, in those that hope in His mercy.

Praise the LORD, O Jerusalem; praise your God, O Zion.

For He has strengthened the bars of your gates; He has blessed your children within you.

He makes peace *in* your borders, *and* fills you with the finest of the wheat.

He sends forth His commandment *upon*

earth: His word runs very swiftly.

He gives snow like wool: He scatters the white frost like ashes.

He casts forth His ice like morsels: who can stand before His cold?

He sends out His word, and melts them: He causes His wind to blow, *and* the waters to flow.

He shows His word unto Jacob, His statutes and His judgments unto Israel.

He has not dealt so with any nation: and *as for His* judgments, they have not known them. Praise the LORD.

## The Hundred and Forty-Eighth Psalm

Praise the LORD. Praise the LORD from the heavens: praise Him in the heights.

Praise Him, all you His angels: praise Him, all His hosts.

Praise Him, you sun and moon: praise Him, all you stars of light.

Praise Him, you heavens of heavens, and you waters that *be* above the heavens.

Let them praise the Name of the LORD: for He commanded, and they were created.

He has also established them for ever and ever: He has made a decree which shall not pass.

Praise the LORD from the earth, you dragons, and all deeps:

Fire, and hail; snow, and vapors; stormy wind fulfilling His word:

Mountains, and all hills; fruitful trees, and all cedars:

Beasts, and all cattle; creeping things, and flying fowl:

Kings of the earth, and all people; princes, and all judges of the earth:

Both young men, and maidens; old men, and children:

Let them praise the name of the LORD: for His Name alone is excellent; His glory *is* above the earth and heaven.

He also exalts the horn of His people, the praise of all His saints; *even* of the children of Israel, a people near unto Him. Praise you the LORD.

**The Hundred and Forty-Ninth Psalm**

Praise the LORD. Sing unto the LORD a new song, *and* His praise in the congregation of saints.

Let Israel rejoice in Him that made him: let the children of Zion be joyful in their King.

Let them praise His Name in the dance: let them sing praises unto Him with the timbrel and harp.

For the LORD takes pleasure in His people: He will beautify the meek with salvation.

Let the saints be joyful in glory: let them sing aloud upon their beds.

*Let* the high *praises* of GOD *be* in their mouth, and a two edged sword in their hand;

To execute vengeance upon the heathen, *and* punishments upon the people;

To bind their kings with chains, and their nobles with fetters of iron;

To execute upon them the judgment

written: this honor has all His saints. Praise you the LORD.

## The Hundred and Fiftieth Psalm

Praise you the LORD. Praise GOD in His sanctuary: praise Him in the firmament of His power.

Praise Him for His mighty acts: praise Him according to His excellent greatness.

Praise Him with the sound of the trumpet: praise Him with the psaltery and harp.

Praise Him with the timbrel and dance: praise Him with stringed instruments and organs.

Praise Him upon the loud cymbals: praise Him upon the high sounding cymbals.

Let every thing that hath breath praise the LORD. Praise you the LORD.

## If one is praying in a Noahide congregation say

May the LORD hear you in the day of trouble; the Name of the God of Jacob defend you;

May the LORD send you help from the sanctuary, and strengthen you out of Zion;

May the LORD remember all your offerings, and accept your burnt sacrifice;

May the LORD grant you according to your own heart, and fulfill all your counsel.

We will rejoice in Your salvation, and in the name of our God we will set up *our* banners: the LORD fulfill all your petitions.

Now I know that the LORD saves His anointed; He will hear Him from His holy heaven with the saving strength of His right hand.

Some *trust* in chariots, and some in horses: but we will remember the name of the LORD our God. (Psalm 20:1-7)

**If one is praying alone say**

Blessed *are* they that dwell in Your house: they will be continually praising You. (Psalm 84:4)

Happy *is that* people, that is in such a case: *yes,* happy *is that* people, whose God *is* the LORD. (Psalm 144:15)

**Continue**

Now I, _____, son/daughter of *[father's name]*, a child of Noah, praise and extol and honor the King of Heaven, all whose works *are* truth, and His ways judgment: and those that walk in pride He is able to abase. (Adapted from Daniel 4:37)

Blessed be the Most High. I praise and honor Him Who lives forever, Whose dominion *is* an everlasting dominion, and His kingdom *is* from generation to generation.

And all the inhabitants of the earth *are* reputed as nothing: and He does according to His will in the army of heaven, and *among* the inhabitants of the earth: and none can stay His hand, or say unto Him, "What have You done?" (Adapted from Daniel 4:34, 31-32)

For the Kingdom belongs to the LORD; He rules over the nations.

And saviors shall come up on Mount Zion to judge the Mount of Esau; and the Kingdom shall be the LORD'S. (Obadiah 1:21)

And the LORD shall be King over all the earth: in that day shall there be one LORD, and His Name one. (Zachariah 14:9)

Praised be Your Name forever, O our King, the great and Holy GOD and King in Heaven and on earth.

For, to You, O LORD our God, it is fitting to offer

songs and hymns, psalms and praises; to proclaim Your strength and dominion, eternity, greatness and power, renown and glory, holiness and kingship; and to express blessings and thanksgivings, from now and for ever.

Blessed are You, LORD God and King, Who is great in praises, God of our thanksgivings, Master of wonders, Who delights in melodious hymns, O King, ever-living God.

## Benediction

Blessed are You, LORD our God, King of the Universe, Who forms light and creates darkness, Who makes peace and creates all things.

In mercy He gives light to the earth and to those who live on it, and in His goodness continually renews the work of creation every day.

How numerous are Your works, O LORD!

You made them all in wisdom. The earth is full of Your creations.

He is the King who alone was exalted before time existed; Who has been praised, glorified and extolled from days of old.

O Eternal GOD, in Your abundant mercies have mercy upon us, for You are the LORD Who grants us strength, the Rock Who affords us refuge, the Shield Who gives us salvation, the Stronghold Who protects us.

The Blessed GOD, great in knowledge, designed and made the rays of the sun; the Beneficent One created them as a glory for His own Name.

He placed the luminaries round about His Majesty. The chiefs of the hosts, all holy ones, exalt the Almighty, proclaiming continually the glory of GOD and His holiness.

Be blessed, LORD our God, for the excellencies of Your handiwork, and for the bright luminaries which You have made. May they glorify You forever.

Be blessed, O our Rock, our King and Redeemer, Creator of the holy beings.

Praised be Your Name for ever, O our King, Creator of the ministering angels, all of whom stand in the heights of the universe, and proclaim with awe, in unison and aloud, the words of the Living God and Eternal King.

All of them are beloved, all of them are pure, all of them are mighty, all of them perform with awe and reverence the will of their Maker.

All of them open their mouths in holiness and purity, with song and melody, and bless, praise, glorify and revere, sanctify and ascribe sovereignty to The Name of the great, mighty and awesome God and King; holy is He.

And they all take upon themselves the yoke of the Kingdom of Heaven one from the other; and give leave to one another to sanctify their Maker. In tranquil spirit, with pure speech and holy melody, they all respond in unison, exclaiming with awe: Holy, Holy, Holy is the Lord of Hosts: the whole earth is full of His glory. Then the Living Beings and the Holy Cherubim, rising with a roaring noise toward the Seraphim, in turn utter praise and say: Blessed be the glory of the LORD from His place.

To the blessed GOD they offer pleasant melodies; to the King, the Living and Eternal God, they utter hymns and proclaim praises. For He alone performs mighty deeds and creates new things; He is the Lord of battles.

He sows righteousness, and causes salvation to flourish; He creates remedies, and is revered through praises. He is the Master of wonders, and in His goodness renews the creation continually every day, as it is said, [Give thanks] to Him who made the great lights, for His loving kindness endures forever.

O cause a new light to shine over Zion, and may we all be worthy soon to enjoy its brightness.

Blessed are You, LORD Creator of the heavenly lights.

Behold, I know that *there is* no God in all the earth except in Israel! (2 Kings 5:15)

## Shema

*We, as Observant Noahides, no matter what our differences of culture from around the globe, share the same origins back to Adam. When we individually or collectively choose to do and accept the ways of GOD as defined by Torah, with Israel as our Teacher-Priests, we link our destiny to that of Israel. Therefore, it is appropriate to confirm our solidarity by saying the Shema along with Israel.*

Hear O Israel, the LORD our God, the LORD is One. (Deuteronomy 6:4)

*The next paragraph is traditionally said in a whisper.*

Blessed be His Name Whose Glorious Kingdom is forever and ever!

And the LORD God commanded the man, saying, "Of every tree of the garden you may freely eat." (Genesis 2:16)

But flesh with the life thereof, *which is* the blood thereof, you shall not eat. (Genesis 9:4)

And these words, which I command you this day, shall be in your heart: And you shall teach them diligently unto your children, and shall talk of them when you sit in your house, and when you walk by the way, and when you lie down, and when you rise up. (Deuteronomy 6:6-7)

The law of the LORD *is* perfect, converting the soul: the testimony of the LORD *is* sure, making wise the simple.

The statutes of the LORD *are* right, rejoicing the heart: the commandment of the LORD *is* pure, enlightening the eyes.

The fear of the LORD *is* clean, enduring for ever: the judgments of the LORD *are* true *and* righteous altogether.

More to be desired *are they* than gold, yes, than much fine gold: sweeter also than honey and the honeycomb.

Moreover by them is Your servant warned: *and* in keeping of them *there is* great reward.

Who can understand *his* errors? Cleanse me from secret *faults*.

Keep back Your servant also from presumptuous *sins;* let them not have dominion over me: then shall I be upright, and I shall be innocent from the great transgression. (Psalm 19:7-13)

*Here ends the Offerings*

*Personal Notes*

*Offerings*

*Service From the Heart*

*Communal Prayers*

*Make a joyful noise unto the LORD, all you lands.*

*Serve the LORD with gladness: come before His presence with singing.*

Psalm 100:1-2

# *Communal Prayers*

## Invitation to Worship

### The Hundredth Psalm

Psalm of Thanksgiving

*Responsive Reading*

**Leader**

Make a joyful noise unto the LORD, all you lands.

Serve the LORD with gladness: come before His presence with singing.

**Response**

Know you that the LORD He *is* God: *it is* He *that* has made us, and not we ourselves; *we are* His people, and the sheep of His pasture.

## Leader

Enter into His gates with thanksgiving, *and* into His courts with praise: be thankful unto Him, *and* bless His Name.

## Response

For the LORD *is* good; His mercy *is* everlasting; and His truth *endures* to all generations.

## Prayer

O LORD, open my lips; and my mouth shall show forth Your praise. (Psalm 51:15)

*Some take three symbolic steps forward.*

## GOD's Covenant

Blessed *[some bend the knees, bow forward at the waist]* are You *[some bow at the head then rise up]*, LORD our God, King of the Nations, Who is the God of Abraham, the God of Isaac, and the God of Jacob; the great, mighty and revered GOD.

The Most High GOD, Who bestows loving kindness, Who is the Creator of all things, Who maintains His covenant with the Children of Israel, and in love will bring a Redeemer to the whole world for His Name's sake.

I praise You LORD for Israel, who teaches us of Your Great Name, Your mighty hand, and Your outstretched arm. O King, our Help, our Savior, and our Shield, our worship is to You alone, in the merit of our forefather Noah.

**On Rosh Hashanah add**

Remember us for life, O King Who desires life, inscribe us in the Book of Life, for Your sake, O Living GOD.

Let our prayers be heard before You, as we are made in Your likeness, to do Your will, that we may merit life in the World-to-Come.

Blessed *[some bend the knees, bow forward at the waist]* are You, the Holy King *[bow at the head then rise]*, LORD, Shield of Abraham the father of all nations.

## GOD's Might

You, LORD are mighty forever; You revive the dead; You have the power to save. You sustain the living with kindness; You revive the dead with great mercy.

You support the falling, heal the sick, set free the bound, and keep faith with those that sleep in the dust.

There is none like You, O Master of mighty deeds. There is nothing that can resemble You--a King who puts to death and restores to life and causes salvation to flourish.

### On Rosh Hashanah add

Who is like You, Father of mercy, Who in mercy remembers His creations unto life!

### Continue

Yes, You are sure to revive the dead.

Blessed are You, LORD, Who revives the dead.

## GOD's Holiness

You are holy, and Your Name is holy, and the holy ones praise You daily.

Blessed are You, LORD the *Holy GOD.

**\*On Rosh Hashanah say**

Holy King

## Knowledge

*Rabbi Nissim Gaon wrote in the introduction to his commentary on the Talmud that all commandments that are dependent on logic and understanding of the heart are incumbent on every human being. We find, for example that in spite of the other serious crimes, violations of the seven laws, that the inhabitants of Sodom were guilty of committing, the prophet Habakkuk states that it was destroyed because they did not practice charity. This is not one of the seven laws but it is logical. Knowledge, understanding, and discernment are important for fulfilling the many obligations that are not mentioned in the seven laws.*

> They are also important for fulfillment of the seven laws. (Rabbi Yechial Sitzman)

You favor man with knowledge, and teach mortals understanding.

O favor us with knowledge, understanding and discernment from You, so that we may fulfill the Commandments that You have given us.

Blessed are You, LORD gracious Giver of knowledge.

**Repentance**

Cause us to return, O our Father, to fulfill our commandments that You commanded us; draw us near, O our King, to Your service, and bring us back in perfect repentance to Your presence.

Blessed are You, LORD, Who delights in repentance.

## Forgiveness

Forgive us, O our Father, for we have sinned; pardon us, O our King, for we have transgressed, for You pardon and forgive.

Blessed are You, LORD, Who is gracious and forgives repeatedly.

## Redemption

Look upon our affliction and approve our cause, and redeem us speedily for Your Name's sake, for You are a mighty Redeemer.

Blessed are You, LORD the Redeemer of Israel and all humanity.

## Healing

Heal us, O LORD, and we shall be healed; save us and we shall be saved, for You are our praise.

O grant healing to all our ailments.

May it be Your will, LORD our God, speedily to send a perfect healing from heaven, a healing of soul and body unto *[person's name]* son/daughter of *[father's name]* among the sick of Israel and the nations. For You Almighty King, are a faithful and merciful Healer.

Blessed are You, LORD Healer of the Sick.

## Prosperity

*We should only pray for what we think we need, for example: In the Middle East during the summer one should not pray for rain, because it would damage grain crops. In certain climates snow is useful or needed for agriculture – one could add "snow", like: Give dew, rain and snow for blessing over the entire face of the land. (Rabbi Yechiel Sitzman)*

## For Times and Places Where There is a Natural Dry Season (not a drought)

Bless for us, our God, this year and all its varieties of its produce for our good.

Bestow abundant blessing on the face of the earth,

and satisfy us with Your goodness, and bless our years like the best years.

Blessed are You, LORD, Who blesses the years.

**For Times and Places When Rain is Needed**

Bless for our benefit, LORD our God, this year, and every sort of its produce – for the good.

Give dew and rain in due season for blessing over the entire face of the land. Quench the thirst of the face of the earth and satiate the entire world from Your bounty. Fill our hands from Your blessings and from the wealth of Your gifts.

Protect and save this year from all evil, from all types of destruction, and from all types of tribulation. Create for it good hope and a peaceful ending.

Take pity and have mercy upon it and upon all its grain and fruit, and bless it with rains of goodwill, blessing and benevolence, and may its end be that of life, contentment and peace as other good years – for blessings, for You are GOD, good and beneficent, Who blesses the years.

Blessed are You, LORD, Who blesses the years.

## For All Seasons

May each grain and fruit be blessed in plenty in its season so that man will be contented and come to peace and happiness.

Blessed are You, LORD, Who blesses the seasons.

## Ingathering of the Israelites

Sound the great trumpet for the freedom of Your People Israel. Raise the ensign to gather the exiles of Israel, and may we merit this prophecy, "We will go with you, for we have heard that GOD is with you" (Zechariah 8:23) at its appointed time.

Remember me, O LORD, with the favor *that You bear unto* Your people: O visit me with Your salvation;

That I may see the good of Your chosen, that I may

rejoice in the gladness of Your nation, that I may glory with Your inheritance. (Psalm 106:4-5)

Blessed are You, LORD, Who gathers the dispersed of His People Israel.

## Justice

Restore the Judges as when Your Temple stood, and remove from us all dispute and sorrow, that all of mankind may live in peace, to know Your Seven Laws for Humanity.

Blessed are You, LORD the *King Who loves righteousness and justice.

**\*On Rosh Hashanah say**

King of justice.

## Against the Enemies of Israel

Let there be no hope for slanderers, and for all those who disseminate atheistic doctrines and let all wickedness perish in an instant.

May all Your enemies be speedily cut down.

May You speedily uproot and crush, cast down and humble the dominion of arrogance, speedily and in our days.

Blessed are You, LORD, Who destroys the enemies and humbles the arrogant.

**For the Righteous**

May Your tender mercies, LORD our God, be stirred towards the righteous and the pious, towards the elders of Your People, the House of Israel, towards the remnant of their Sages, towards the righteous proselytes, and also towards us, who have pledged to observe the Eternal Covenant that You made with Noah our Father.

Grant a good reward to all who truly trust in Your Name. Set our lot like unto them forever; and may we never be put to shame, for we trust in You.

Blessed are You, LORD the stay and trust of the righteous.

## The Rebuilding of Jerusalem

And to Jerusalem, Your City, return in mercy, and dwell therein as You have spoken; rebuild it soon in our days as an everlasting building, and speedily set up therein the Throne of David.

## On the Ninth of Av add

Console, LORD, our God, the mourners of Zion and the mourners of Jerusalem, and the City that is destroyed, debased and desolate. She sits without her children with her head covered in shame like a barren woman who has never given birth.

Legions have devoured and possessed her and they have put Your People, Israel, to the sword, and they have willfully murdered the pious ones of the Supreme One.

Therefore, Zion weeps bitterly, and Jerusalem gives forth her voice, "My heart!"

My heart grieves for their murdered! For You, LORD--with fire did You consume her and with fire You are destined to rebuild her, as it is written, "I, says the LORD, will be unto her a wall of fire round about, and will be the glory in the midst of her." (Zechariah 2:5)

Blessed are You, LORD, Who consoles Zion with the rebuilding of Jerusalem.

**Continue**

Blessed are You, LORD, Who rebuilds Jerusalem.

**Kingdom of David**

Speedily cause the offspring of Your servant David to flourish, and let his honor be exalted by Your saving power, for we also wait all day for Your salvation.

Blessed are You, LORD, Who causes the strength of salvation to flourish.

**Response to Prayer**

Hear our voice, LORD our God; merciful Father, have pity and be compassionate with us, and accept our prayer with compassion and with favor – for You are GOD,

Who hears prayers and supplications. From before You, our King, do not turn us away empty handed. Be gracious to us and respond to us and hear our prayer.

### If Fasting During the Fasts of Tevet, Esther, Seventeenth Tammuz, Gedaliah and Av add

*Fasting is not required of B'nai Noah. But, if one wishes to fast as an act of solidarity with Israel, keep in mind that fasting means abstention from all food and drink including water. (Rabbi Michael Katz)*

Answer us, our Father, our King, answer us, on this day of fasting, for Your People Israel is in great distress.

Do not pay heed to our wickedness, and, our King, do not ignore our plea.

Please be near to the cries of the supplicants, so that You will answer even before we call to You, and You will hear even while we still speak, as it is stated, "And it shall come to pass, that before they call, I will answer; and while they are yet speaking, I will hear." (Isaiah 65:24)

For You, LORD redeem, save, respond, and show

compassion in every time of trouble and distress.

**Continue**

For You hear the prayer of every mouth.

Blessed are You, LORD, Who hears prayer.

**Restoration of the Temple Service**

We await the day when You will restore Your Temple, that we may joyfully bring before You our sacrifices there as it is written, "Even them will I bring to My Holy Mountain, and make them joyful in My House of Prayer: their burnt offerings and their sacrifices *shall be* accepted upon My altar; for My house shall be called a house of prayer for all people." (Isaiah 56:7)

Restore, therefore, the service to Your Most Holy House, and receive in love and with favor the fire-offerings of Israel and their prayer.

May the service of Your People Israel always be acceptable to You.

## On the New Moon

Heavenly Father, Lord of the Universe, as the heavens proclaim Your glory, so the New Moon proclaims Your providence. Even when we do not see Your guiding hand, You will still emerge from the darkness to renew our knowledge and love for You.

Remove all darkness and obscurity from the earth and restore Your People Israel with the coming of the Anointed Redeemer. For we wait only upon You.

## Continue

And may our eyes behold Your return in mercy to Zion, so that the redeemed shall walk in it; and the ransomed of the Lord shall return, and come with shouting unto Zion, crowned with joy everlasting.

They shall attain joy and gladness, while sorrow and sighing flee.

May it come to fulfillment that:

Many people shall go and say, come and let us go up to the mountain of the LORD, to the house of the God of Jacob; and He will teach us of His ways, and we will walk in His paths: for out of Zion shall go forth the law, and the word of the LORD from Jerusalem. (Isaiah 2:3)

Blessed are You, LORD, Who restores His divine presence to Zion.

**Thanksgiving**

We *[some bend the knees, bow forward at the waist]* acknowledge that You *[bow at the head then rise up]* are the LORD our God, forever and ever.

**Noahides who have pledged to keep the Covenant add**

From this generation,

**Noahides who are descended from parents of the Covenant add**

From generation to generation,

**Continue**

You will be the Rock of our lives, and the Shield of our salvation.

We will give thanks to You and declare Your praise, for our lives which are committed to Your care, for our souls which are entrusted to You, for Your miracles which are daily with us, and for Your wonders and favors which are with us at all times: evening, morning and noon.

O Beneficent One, Your mercies never fail; O Merciful One, Your loving kindness never ceases. We will always put our hope in You.

*Continue on page 92 or with one of the following.*

## On the Festival of Passover add

On this day, You delivered Your first-born, Israel, out of the slavery of Egypt. With signs and wonders, You caused Your hand to move against the tyranny, injustice and cruelty of Egypt. You taught us that true freedom comes from serving You.

Release our bonds and cause us to serve You with all our heart, with all our soul, with all our might, that we may, in humility, attain the qualities like that of a High Priest of Israel.

*Continue on page 92.*

## On Shavuot (Pentecost) add

On this day, You gave the Torah in its entirety, so that Israel may become a Kingdom of Priests, a Holy Nation and a Light unto the Nations. Through the authority of Moses, Chief of all the Prophets of those who preceded him and after him, we receive the Laws of Noah.

May the Seven Laws be known to the nations speedily and soon, so that all nations, together with Israel, will serve You with one pure voice and one united heart, that Your Name will be called "One".

*Continue on page 92.*

**On Rosh Hashanah (New Year) add**

On this day, You created the First Man Adam. It is also the birthday of the world.

We thank You, LORD our God, that we are privileged to know You and serve You through the Seven Laws You ordained for us.

May You be acknowledged as King and Creator of Man by all mankind speedily and soon.

On this day, You open the Gates of Repentance and Righteousness. Through the example of Your People Israel, though our good deeds be little, may our small acts of mercy, our strivings for justice, our fasts, penance and prayers, be pleasing before You, that we may merit life in the World-to-Come, and in the Book of Life, blessing, peace, good livelihood, salvation, consolation, and good decrees, may we be remembered and inscribed before You; we, and Your entire People Israel, for a good life and for peace.

*Continue on page 92.*

### During Sukkot (Feast of Booths) add

On this day, we learn how the remnant of the nations will one day come before You, acknowledging You as their King, as it is written by the Prophet Zechariah,

> And it shall come to pass, *that* every one that is left of all the nations which came against Jerusalem shall even go up from year to year to worship the King, the LORD of hosts, and to keep the Feast of Tabernacles.

> And it shall be, *that* whoso will not come up of *all* the families of the earth unto Jerusalem to

worship the King, the LORD of hosts, even upon them shall be no rain.

And if the family of Egypt go not up, and come not, that *have* no *rain;* there shall be the plague, wherewith the LORD will smite the heathen that come not up to keep the Feast of Tabernacles.

This shall be the punishment of Egypt, and the punishment of all nations that come not up to keep the Feast of Tabernacles. (Zechariah 14:16-19)

We thank You that You have privileged us by revealing to us the paths of life known as the Seven Laws of Noah.

As we come from the many lands to learn Your Laws, may You spare us from the fate of those nations who would harm Your Nation.

May You spare us from being victims of their tyranny and control.

May You spare us from their dictates of evil decrees. May we, who have heeded Your call, be under Your divine protection.

Cause us to serve You with a whole and perfect heart.

*Continue on page 92.*

## On Simchat Torah (Rejoicing of the Torah) add

On this day, Your Children Israel rejoice in their sacred inheritance, the Torah.

May we, like them, rejoice heartily in our portion, the Laws of Noah.

May our observance bring us length of days and happiness.

May the Lights of the Rainbow illuminate from within us when we take joy and delight in Your Commandments.

Blessed are You, LORD, Who elevates our lives through the Seven Laws of Noah.

*Continue on page 92.*

**On Chanukah add**

We, together with Your People Israel, wish to express our thanks for the miracles, for the redemption, for the mighty deeds, and for the victories in battle, which You performed for Israel in those days at this season.

Through this remembrance, may the enemies of Israel be warned that any effort to annihilate Your People will bring doom upon themselves.

On this day, the wicked Greek Kingdom rose up against Israel to make them forget Your Torah and violate the decrees of Your will.

They made wicked decrees from the arrogance of their hearts, attempting to place their human reason in rivalry to Your revealed wisdom, the Torah of Israel, and the Seven Laws which they were commanded to observe.

But You gave aid to Matityahu the Priest and his sons, and You stood by them in the time of their distress, waged their battles, defended their rights, and avenged the wrong done to them.

You delivered the mighty into the hands of the weak, the many into the hands of the few, the impure into the hands of the pure, and the wanton sinners into the hands of those who occupy themselves with Your Torah.

You made for Yourself a great and holy Name in Your world, and effected deliverance and redemption to this very day, for then Your Children entered the shrine of Your Temple and cleansed it, purified Your Sanctuary, and kindled lights in Your holy courtyard.

O Almighty GOD, the Greeks sinned because they had no fear of You in their hearts, but we who know Your Seven Holy Laws are ready to walk with You and to understand Your wisdom.

Just as You gave strength to Israel to be a priesthood to us and to all the world, fill the hearts of all the righteous of the nations who turn from the sinful way, that the rule of evil may be abolished from the earth. For on that day, You will be revealed as the only God, and Your Name will be One over all the nations.

Amen, may this be Your will.

**On Purim add**

We, together with Your People Israel, wish to express our thanks for the miracles, for the redemption, for the mighty deeds, and for the victories in battle, which You performed for Israel in those days at this season.

Through this remembrance, may the enemies of Israel be warned that any effort to annihilate Your People will bring doom upon themselves.

It was in the days of Mordechai and Esther, in Shushan the capital, when the wicked Haman rose up against them and sought to destroy, slay and exterminate all the Jews, young and old, infants and women, in one day, on the thirteenth day of the twelfth month, which is the month of Adar, and to plunder their possessions, that You in Your great mercy frustrated his counsel and upset his design, and caused his scheming to recoil upon his own head, so that he and his sons were hanged on the gallows.

**Continue**

For all these wonders may Your Name be blessed and exalted continually, O our King, forever and ever.

Let all living beings ever thank You, and praise Your Name in truth, O GOD, for You have always been our salvation and our help.

Blessed *[bend the knees, bow forward at the waist]* are You *[bow at the head then rise]*, LORD, Whose Name is the Beneficent One, and to Whom it is fitting to give thanks.

**Peace**

Grant peace, goodness and blessing, life, grace and kindness, and compassion over us and over all Israel, Your Nation.

Bless us all as one, our Father, with the light of Your countenance. You, LORD our God, gave us the Torah of the Seven Laws and life, love of kindness, righteousness and compassion, blessing, and peace.

Let all living beings ever thank You, and praise Your Name in truth, O GOD, for You have always been our salvation and our help.

Blessed *[some bend the knees, then bow forward at the waist]* are You *[bow at the head then rise]*, LORD, Whose Name is the Beneficent One, and to Whom it is fitting to give thanks.

Blessed are You, LORD, Who blesses humanity with peace.

## Prayer for Parents

May GOD, Who richly blessed Noah and his family, bestow a blessing on my father and mother.

May they have a long life, a life of peace, a life of good, a life of blessing, a life of sustenance, a life of bodily vigor, a life of affluence and honor, a life imbued with the love of Your Torah of the Seven Laws, a life in which You will fulfill all the aspirations of their heart.

Because they are the pillars of our household.

**Prayer for Children**

May the LORD, the Most High God, Maker of heaven and earth bless *[name each child]* to walk with Him among the Righteous of the Nations, now and for evermore.

**Prayer of Sustenance**

My help *comes* from the LORD, Who made heaven and earth. (Psalm 121:2)

Cast your burden upon the LORD, and He shall sustain you…. (Psalm 55:22)

Mark the innocent *man,* and behold the upright: for the end of *that* man *is* peace. (Psalm 37:37)

Trust in the LORD, and do good; *so* shall you dwell in the land, and surely you shall be fed. (Psalm 37:3)

Behold, GOD *is* my salvation; I will trust, and not be afraid: for the LORD God *is* my strength and *my* song; He also is become my salvation. (Isaiah 12:2)

O Sovereign of the Universe, in Your Holy Words it is written, saying, "he that trusts in the LORD, mercy shall compass him about." (Psalm 32:10)

O LORD, God of Truth, send blessing and prosperity upon all the work of my hands, for I trust in You that You will so bless me through my occupation and calling, that I may be enabled to support myself and the members of my household with ease and not with pain, by lawful and not by unlawful means, unto life and peace.

In me also let the Scripture be fulfilled, "Cast your burden upon the LORD, and He shall sustain you...." (Psalm 55:22)

## Concluding Prayer

Sovereign of all worlds! It is revealed and known to You that we would like to act according to Your will, but what prevents us?

Negative passions and the oppression of worldly powers.

May it be Your will to save us from the grip of their power, and then we shall be penitent and heed the Laws which emanate from Your will with a full heart.

O my GOD, before I was formed I was without worth, and now that I have been formed I am as though I had not been formed. Like dust am I in life, how much more so when I die.

In Your presence, I am as a vessel filled with shame and confusion.

May it be Your will, O LORD my God, that I sin no more, and as to the sins I have committed before You, purge them from me in Your great compassion, but not through grievous suffering and disease.

Let the words of my mouth, and the meditation of my heart, be acceptable in Your sight, O LORD, my strength, and my redeemer. (Psalm 19:14)

*Some take three steps back, while head still bowed forward, turn to the left, bow and say*

May He Who establishes peace in His realm on high,

*Straighten the body at center, turn to the right, bow to the right and say*

Establish peace for us,

*Straighten the body at center, bow forward and say*

And for all Israel!

*Straighten the body and say*

Say to this, Amen!

**Continue**

May it be Your will, O LORD our God, the God of our forefather Noah, the God of Abraham, Isaac and Israel, that the House of Prayer for all nations be speedily rebuilt in our days, and grant us our share in Your Torah.

And towards that House we will worship You with reverence, as in the days of old and as in former years.

Then the elevation-offerings of all the nations will be pleasing to the LORD as in the days of old and as in former years.

**Personal or National Distress**

### The Twentieth Psalm

To the chief Musician, A Psalm of David.

May the LORD hear you in the day of trouble; the Name of the God of Jacob defend you;

May He send you help from the sanctuary, and strengthen you out of Zion;

May He remember all your offerings, and accept your burnt sacrifice;

May He grant you according to your own heart, and fulfill all your counsel.

We will rejoice in Your salvation, and in the Name of our God we will set up *our* banners: the LORD fulfill all your petitions.

Now know I that the LORD saves His anointed; He will hear him from His holy heaven with the saving strength of His right hand.

Some *trust* in chariots, and some in horses: but we will remember the Name of the LORD our God.

They are brought down and fallen: but we are raised up, and stand upright.

Save, LORD: let the King hear us when we call.

**For the Welfare of Israel**

### The Eighty-Third Psalm

A Song *or* Psalm of Asaph.

Keep not Your silence, O GOD: hold not Your peace, and be not still, O GOD.

For, lo, Your enemies make a tumult: and they that hate You have lifted up their head.

They have taken crafty counsel against Your people, and consulted against Your hidden ones.

They have said, Come, and let us cut them off from *being* a nation; that the name of Israel may be no more in remembrance.

For they have consulted together with one consent: they are confederate against You:

The tabernacles of Edom, and the Ishmaelites; of Moab, and the Hagarenes;

Gebal, and Ammon, and Amalek; the Philistines with the inhabitants of Tyre;

Assur also is joined with them: they have helped the children of Lot.

Do unto them as *unto* the Midianites; as *to* Sisera, as *to* Jabin, at the brook of Kison:

*Which* perished at Endor: they became *as* dung for the earth.

Make their nobles like Oreb, and like Zeeb: yes, all their princes as Zebah, and as Zalmunna:

Who said, Let us take to ourselves the houses of GOD in possession.

O my GOD, make them like a wheel; as the stubble before the wind.

As the fire burns a wood, and as the flame sets the mountains on fire;

So persecute them with Your tempest, and make them afraid with Your storm.

Fill their faces with shame; that they may seek Your Name, O LORD.

Let them be confounded and troubled for ever; yes, let them be put to shame, and perish:

That *men* may know that You, whose Name alone *is* LORD, *are* the most high over all the earth.

**Concluding Psalm**

### The Sixty-Seventh Psalm

To the chief Musician on Neginoth,

A Psalm *or* Song.

GOD be merciful unto us, and bless us; *and* cause His face to shine upon us;

That Your way may be known upon earth, Your saving health among all nations.

Let the people praise You, O GOD; let all the people praise You.

O let the nations be glad and sing for joy: for You shall judge the people righteously, and govern the nations upon earth.

Let the people praise You, O GOD; let all the people praise You.

*Then* shall the earth yield her increase; *and* GOD, *even* our own God, shall bless us.

GOD shall bless us; and all the ends of the earth shall fear Him.

Lead me, O LORD, in Your righteousness because of my enemies; make Your way straight before my face. (Psalm 5:8)

*But* surely GOD has heard *me;* He has attended to the voice of my prayer.

Blessed *be* GOD, which has not turned away my prayer, nor His mercy from me. (Psalm 66:19-20)

*Here ends the Communal Prayers*

*Personal Notes*

## Communal Prayers

*Service From the Heart*

*Evening Reflections*

*And all flesh will call upon Your Name, and all who now dwell in confusion will recognize and know You, for to You every knee will bend and every tongue will swear, and all will take upon themselves the yoke of Your Kingdom.*

# *Evening Reflections*

## Meditations

- What were the major events of your day?
- Did you cause anyone any needless pain today?
- What acts of kindness have you done today?
- Are you satisfied with your use of time today?
- Did you get angry at anyone today?
- What would you have done differently?
- Are you satisfied with your spiritual growth today?
- Did you spend time studying Torah today?

*(From Rabbi Pliskin's* Gateway to Self-Knowledge, *1986, p. 189)*

## Bedtime Prayer

Blessed are You, LORD our God, King of the Universe Who causes the bonds of sleep to fall upon my eyes, and slumber upon my eyelids, and brings sight to the pupil of the eye.

May it be Your will, LORD, my God, that You may lay me down to sleep in peace and arouse me to a good life and to peace.

Give me my portion in Your Torah of the Seven Laws; help me to be observant of Your Laws and do not allow me to commit transgressions.

Do not lead me to sin, nor to be tested, nor to shame.

Let the good inclination govern me instead of the evil inclination.

Rescue me from evil and from serious illness.

Let me not be frightened by bad dreams or evil thoughts.

Let my offspring be perfect before You.

Illuminate my eyes lest I sleep the sleep of death.

Blessed are You, LORD, Who illuminates the entire world with His glory.

Behold, now I know that *there is* no God in all the earth, but in Israel. (2nd Kings 5:15)

**Shema**

*We as Observant Noahides no matter what our differences of culture from around the globe, share the same origins back to Adam. When we individually or collectively choose to do and accept the ways of GOD, as defined by Torah, with Israel as our Teacher-Priests, we link our destiny to that of Israel. Therefore, it is appropriate to confirm our solidarity by saying the Shema along with Israel.*

Hear O Israel, the LORD our God, the LORD is One. (Deuteronomy 6:4)

*Next paragraph is traditionally said in a whisper.*

Blessed be His Name Whose Glorious Kingdom is forever and ever!

And the LORD God commanded the man, saying, "Of every tree of the garden you may freely eat." (Genesis 2:16)

"But flesh with the life thereof, *which is* the blood thereof, you shall not eat." (Genesis 9:4)

"And these words, which I command you this day, shall be in your heart: And you shall teach them diligently unto your children, and shall talk of them when you sit in your house, and when you walk by the way, and when you lie down, and when you rise up." (Deuteronomy 6:6-7)

**Continue**

*By Reb Yirmeyahu Bindman*

Heavenly Father, Creator of day and night, Who appointed the day for the work of man and the night for his rest, accept my soul into Your hands while I sleep.

Cleanse me from the cares of the day, forgive my transgressions, and restore me for Your service when the next day dawns.

May all my deeds be weighed in Your estimation, and the accounting be kept before me.

For in Your sight everything is according to the deeds of man.

May my dreams be pleasant, and may they restore my soul from its earthly happenings, to be pure once again as it was breathed into me.

Bring Your Redeemer today, that Your people Israel may be returned to their land and the Law go out once more from Jerusalem.

"For then will I give the people a pure language, that they may all call upon the name of the LORD, to serve Him with one consent." (Zephaniah 3:9)

And all flesh will call upon Your Name, and all who now dwell in confusion will recognize and know You, for to You every knee will bend and every tongue will swear, and all will take upon themselves the yoke of Your Kingdom.

*Here ends the Evening Reflections*

*Personal Notes*

*Evening Reflections*

*Service From the Heart*

*Remembering the Seventh Day*

*And GOD blessed the Seventh Day, and sanctified it: because that in it He had rested from all His work which GOD created and made.*

*Genesis 2:3*

# Remembering the Seventh Day

## Lighting the Candles

*To make a distinction between B'nai Noah and B'nai Israel, we light the candles in honor of the Seventh Day after sundown.*

## Prayer

*Traditionally, this prayer is said by the Woman of the House, but may be said by any member of the household in her absence.*

You are blessed and praised LORD, our God, Ruler of the Universe, Who enlightens the world and makes it holy by providing commandments to guide and elevate mankind.

May it be Your will, LORD God, that the light of Your commandments will enlighten the whole world and Your Tabernacle be rebuilt soon in our time, and that all the world comes to Your Torah, that we may serve You there reverently.

May it be Your will, GOD, Creator of the Universe and God of all Humanity, that You show favor to all Your servants and in particular to me *[my husband, my sons, my daughters, my father, my mother]* and all my relatives; and that You grant us a long and good life in service to You; that You remember us with beneficent memory and blessing; that You consider us with a consideration of salvation and compassion; that You bless us with great blessings; that You make our household complete; and that You cause Your Presence to dwell among us.

Privilege *[me/us]* to raise children and grandchildren who are wise and understanding, who love and fear You, GOD, that they may grow up to be people of truth, attached to You, GOD, our God and Redeemer, that they may illuminate the world with good and righteous deeds, and that each of their labors be in service of You, our God, Creator of the Universe.

Please hear our supplications at this time and let Your countenance shine on us all.

## Psalm 1

Blessed *is* the man that walks not in the counsel of the ungodly, nor stands in the way of sinners, nor sits in the seat of the scornful.

But his delight *is* in the Law of the LORD; and in his law does he meditate day and night.

And he shall be like a tree planted by the rivers of water, that brings forth his fruit in his season; his leaf also shall not wither; and whatsoever he does shall prosper.

The ungodly *are* not so: but *are* like the chaff which the wind drives away.

Therefore the ungodly shall not stand in the judgment, nor sinners in the congregation of the righteous.

For the LORD knows the way of the righteous: but the way of the ungodly shall perish.

## Woman of Valor

### Proverbs 31:10-31

Who can find a virtuous woman? for her price *is* far above rubies.

The heart of her husband safely trusts in her, so that he shall have no need of spoil.

She will do him good and not evil all the days of her life.

She seeks wool, and flax, and works willingly with her hands.

She is like the merchants' ships; she brings her food from afar.

She rises also while it is yet night, and gives meat to her household, and a portion to her maidens.

She considers a field, and buys it: with the fruit of her hands she plants a vineyard.

She girds her loins with strength, and strengthens her arms.

She perceives that her merchandise *is* good: her candle goes not out by night.

She lays her hands to the spindle, and her hands hold the distaff.

She stretches out her hand to the poor; yes, she reaches forth her hands to the needy.

She is not afraid of the snow for her household: for all her household *are* clothed with scarlet.

She makes herself coverings of tapestry; her clothing *is* silk and purple.

Her husband is known in the gates, when he sits among the elders of the land.

She makes fine linen, and sells *it;* and delivers girdles unto the merchant.

Strength and honor *are* her clothing; and she shall rejoice in time to come.

She opens her mouth with wisdom; and in her tongue *is* the law of kindness.

She looks well to the ways of her household, and eats not the bread of idleness.

Her children arise up, and call her blessed; her husband *also,* and he praises her.

Many daughters have done virtuously, but you excel them all.

Favor *is* deceitful, and beauty *is* vain: *but* a woman *that* fears the LORD, she shall be praised.

Give her of the fruit of her hands; and let her own works praise her in the gates.

## Blessing of the Children

*Many authorities maintain that only a Kohen (Priest) is permitted to use both hands. The concern is that a layman may be confused with a Kohen when he utters this Priestly blessing. Hence, there needs to be a distinction and the practice is that someone other than a Kohen places only one hand on the child's head. (Rabbi Michael Katz)*

*Parent places right hand on child's head and says*

May GOD, the Most High God, Maker of Heaven and Earth bless you, *[child's name]*, to walk with Him among the Righteous of the Nations, May GOD watch over you, shine His face toward you, show you favor, and grant you peace both now and forever more.

## Blessing of the Wine

*Recited over a full cup of wine or grape juice.*

And on the Seventh Day, GOD ended His work which He had made; and He rested on the Seventh Day from all His work which

He had made.

And GOD blessed the Seventh Day, and sanctified it: because that in it He had rested from all His work which GOD created and made. (Genesis 2:2-3)

Blessed are You, O LORD our God, King of the Universe, Who creates the fruit of the vine.

We praise You, GOD, for the covenant that You made with Noah after the flood of the earth. We regret and admit that it is You who has been faithful to remember the covenant and us who have forgotten. You are blessed, LORD God, the Sovereign of the Universe, Who remembers the covenant, fulfills His pledge and keeps His word.

**Washing of the Hands**

*The only reason to ask a Ben Noah to wash his/her hands is out of respect for prayers and as a reminder that every person should have hands that are clean from wrong doing toward his fellow man. For these purposes any method of washing hands should suffice. (Rabbi Yoel Schwartz)*

## Suggested Meditation:

### Psalm 24:3-5

Who shall ascend into the hill of the LORD? or who shall stand in His holy place?

He that has clean hands, and a pure heart; who has not lifted up his soul unto vanity, nor sworn deceitfully.

He shall receive the blessing from the LORD, and righteousness from the God of his salvation.

## Blessing of the Bread

Blessed are You, LORD, our God, King of the Universe, Who brings forth bread from the earth.

*Pass the bread and let everyone break off a piece and eat it.*

*Eat the Seventh Day Meal*

## During the Meal

*It is good to discuss Torah between courses: for instance, some discuss the weekly Torah Portion. Songs can also be sung. (See the song section.)*

*Suggestion: Type up some questions and create little "Torah" scrolls with them prior to the Seventh Day. Each person at the table takes a scroll and reads the question on it. One person may answer or the group may discuss the question.*

## After the Meal

### Psalm 92

A Sabbath Psalm

*It is a* good *thing* to give thanks unto the LORD, and to sing praises unto Your name, O Most High:

To show forth Your loving kindness in the morning, and Your faithfulness every night,

Upon an instrument of ten strings, and upon the psaltery; upon the harp with a solemn sound.

For You, LORD have made me glad through Your work: I will triumph in the works of Your hands.

O LORD, how great are Your works! *and* Your thoughts are very deep.

A brutish man knows not; neither does a fool understand this.

When the wicked spring as the grass, and when all the workers of iniquity do flourish; *it is* that they shall be destroyed for ever:

But You, LORD *are most* high for evermore.

For, lo, Your enemies, O LORD, for, lo, Your enemies shall perish; all the workers of iniquity shall be scattered.

But my horn shall You exalt like *the horn of* an unicorn: I shall be anointed with fresh oil.

My eye also shall see *my desire* on my enemies, *and* my ears shall hear *my desire* of the wicked that rise up against me.

The righteous shall flourish like the palm tree: he shall grow like a cedar in Lebanon.

Those that are planted in the House of the LORD shall flourish in the courts of our God.

They shall still bring forth fruit in old age; they shall be fat and flourishing;

To show that the LORD *is* upright: *He is* my rock, and *there is* no unrighteousness in Him.

## Blessing after the Meal

Blessed are You, LORD, our GOD, King of the Universe, Who feeds the whole world with His goodness, pleasantness, grace and mercy.

He gives bread to all flesh, and the world is full of His Mercy.

Due to His great goodness, we have never lacked and will never be in need of food forever.

His great Name feeds and gives everyone his livelihood, does good to everyone, and prepares food for all those that He has created.

*Here ends the Seventh Day Remembrance*

*Personal Notes*

_____

_____

_____

_____

*Service From the Heart*

*Remembering the Seventh Day*

*Service From the Heart*

*Seventh Day*

*Noon Meal*

*We praise You GOD for the covenant that You made with Noah after the flood of the earth. We regret and admit that it is You who has been faithful to remember the covenant and us who have forgotten.*

# Seventh Day Noon Meal

༺☙༻☙༺☙༺☙༺☙༺☙༺☙༺☙༺☙

**Blessing of the Wine**

*Recited over a full cup of wine or grape juice.*

And the evening and the morning were the sixth day. Thus the heavens and the earth were finished, and all the host of them. And on the Seventh Day GOD ended His work which He had made; and He rested on the Seventh Day from all His work which He had made. And GOD blessed the Seventh Day, and sanctified it: because that in it He had rested from all His work which GOD created and made. (Genesis 1:31-2:3)

Blessed are You, O LORD, our God, King of the Universe, Who creates the fruit of the vine.

We praise You, GOD, for the covenant that You made with Noah after the flood of the earth. We regret and admit that it is You who has been faithful to remember the covenant and us who have forgotten. You are blessed, LORD God, the Sovereign of the Universe, who remembers the covenant, fulfills His pledge, and keeps His word.

## Washing of the Hands

### Suggested Meditation

### Psalm 24:3-5

Who shall ascend into the hill of the LORD? Or who shall stand in His holy place?

He that has clean hands, and a pure heart; who has not lifted up his soul unto vanity, nor sworn deceitfully.

He shall receive the blessing from the LORD, and righteousness from the God of his salvation.

## Blessing of the Bread

Blessed are You, LORD, our God, King of the Universe, Who brings forth bread from the earth.

*Pass the bread and let everyone break off a piece and eat it.*

### Eat the Seventh Day Noon Meal

### Here ends the Seventh Day Noon Meal

*Personal Notes*

*Service From the Heart*

*Seventh Day*

*Evening Meal*

*Blessed are You, LORD, our God, King of the Universe, Who brings forth bread from the earth.*

# Seventh Day Evening Meal

ଔଔଔଔଔଔଔଔଔଔ

**Blessing of the Wine**

*Recited over a full cup of wine or grape juice.*

And the evening and the morning were the sixth day. Thus the heavens and the earth were finished, and all the host of them. And on the Seventh Day GOD ended His work which He had made; and He rested on the Seventh Day from all His work which He had made. And GOD blessed the Seventh Day, and sanctified it: because that in it He had rested from all His work which GOD created and made. (Genesis 1:31-2:3)

Blessed are You, O LORD, our God, King of the Universe, Who creates the fruit of the vine.

We praise You, GOD, for the covenant that You made with Noah after the flood of the earth. We regret and admit that it is You who has been faithful to remember the covenant and us who have forgotten. You are blessed, LORD God, the Sovereign of the Universe, Who remembers the covenant, fulfils His pledge and keeps His word.

## Washing of the Hands

### Suggested Meditation:

### Psalm 24:3-5

Who shall ascend into the hill of the LORD? Or who shall stand in His holy place?

He who has clean hands, and a pure heart; who has not lifted up his soul unto vanity, nor sworn deceitfully.

He shall receive the blessing from the LORD, and righteousness from the God of his salvation.

## Blessing of the Bread

Blessed are You, LORD, our God, King of the Universe, Who brings forth bread from the earth.

*Pass the bread and let everyone break off a piece and eat it.*

*Eat the Seventh Day Evening Meal*

## Blessing after the Meal

Blessed are You, LORD, our God, King of the Universe, Who feeds the whole world with His goodness, pleasantness, grace and mercy.

He gives bread to all flesh and the world is full of His Mercy.

Due to His great goodness, we have never lacked and will never be in need of food forever.

His great Name feeds and gives everyone his livelihood, does good to everyone, and prepares food for all those that He has created.

*Here ends the Seventh Day Evening Meal*

## Personal Notes

*Seventh Day Evening Meal*

*Service From the Heart*

# Havdalah

*Blessed are You, O LORD, our God, King of the Universe, Who makes a distinction between the Seventh Day and the regular days of the week, between light and darkness, between Israel and the Nations of the world, and between Jew and Gentile, who together are partners in one Holy objective, to make Your Name One throughout the world.*

# *Havdalah*

## At the Close of the Seventh Day, after Sundown

Behold, GOD *is* my salvation; I will trust, and not be afraid: for the LORD God *is* my strength and *my* song; He also is become my salvation. Therefore with joy shall you draw water out of the wells of salvation. (Isaiah 12:2-3)

Salvation belongs to the LORD. (Psalm 3:8) May Your blessings be upon those who believe in You.

Whoso trusts in the LORD, happy *is* he. (Proverbs 16:20) I will take the cup of salvation, and call upon the name of the LORD. (Psalm 116:13)

## Blessing of the Wine

*Recited over a full cup of wine or grape juice.*

Blessed are You, O LORD, our God, King of the Universe, Who creates the fruit of the vine.

## Sweet Smelling Spices

*Because we feel saddened at the departure of the Seventh Day, we indicate our need to revive our spirits by enjoying aromatic spices.*

Blessed are You, O LORD, our God, King of the Universe, Creator of various kinds of spices.

## For the Flames

*Use multi-wick candle. If possible, a candle with seven wicks, one to represent each of the Seven Laws of Noah.*

Blessed are You, O LORD, our God, King of the Universe, Creator of the lights of fire.

Blessed are You, LORD, our God, King of the

Universe, Creator of the lights of fire, Who taught Adam how to make fire, which is the source of all energy that enables man to make changes in this world.

Blessed are You, O LORD, our God, King of the Universe, Who makes a distinction between the Seventh Day and the regular days of the week, between light and darkness, between Israel and the Nations of the world, and between Jew and Gentile, who together are partners in one Holy objective, to make Your Name One throughout the world.

You are blessed, LORD, who makes a distinction between the sacred and the secular. Amen.

### Here ends Havdalah

(The Remembering the Seventh Day, Seventh Day Noon Meal, Seventh Day Evening Meal, and Havdalah sections constitute a full reprint of *Shabbat: a Celebration for the Non-Jew* © 2002 Oklahoma B'nai Noah Society, portions of which were reprinted with permission from the *B'nai Noah Quarterly* © 2000.)

## Personal Notes

*Havdalah*

*Service From the Heart*

# Songs

*O sing unto the LORD a new song: sing unto the LORD, all the earth.*

*Sing unto the LORD, bless His name; show forth His salvation from day to day.*

*Psalm 96:1-2*

# Songs

*Columns on the left are the English Translation and columns on the right are transliterated Hebrew*

## Hine Ma Tov (How Good and Pleasant it is)

| | |
|---|---|
| Behold, how good and pleasant it is for brothers to dwell together. | Hine ma tov u-ma naim Shevet ahim gam yahad |

## David Melekh Yisrael (David King of Israel)

| | |
|---|---|
| David, King of Israel | David Melekh Yisrael |
| Live, live forever | Hai, hai ve-kayam |

## Haveinu Shalom Aleikhem (We Bring You Peace)

| | |
|---|---|
| We bring you peace, | Haveinu shalom aleikhem |
| We bring you peace, | Haveinu shalom aleikhem |
| We bring you peace, | Haveinu shalom aleikhem |
| We bring you peace, peace, | Haveinu shalom, shalom, |
| Peace, unto you. | Shalom aleikhem |

## Adon Olam (Master of the Universe)

Master of the Universe Who reigned Before any creature was created.

Adon Olam asher malakh Beterem kol yetzer nivra

At the time when all was made by His will, then was His Name proclaimed King.

Le'et na'asa be-heftzo kol Azay melekh shemo nikera.

And after all things shall cease to be The Awesome One will reign alone.

He was, He is, and He shall be in glory.

Ve-aharei Kikhlot Ha-kol Levado Yimlokh Nora

Ve-hu Haya, Ve-hu Hovve Ve-hu Yiheye Be-tif ara

*Additional Songs*

*Songs*

## Service From the Heart

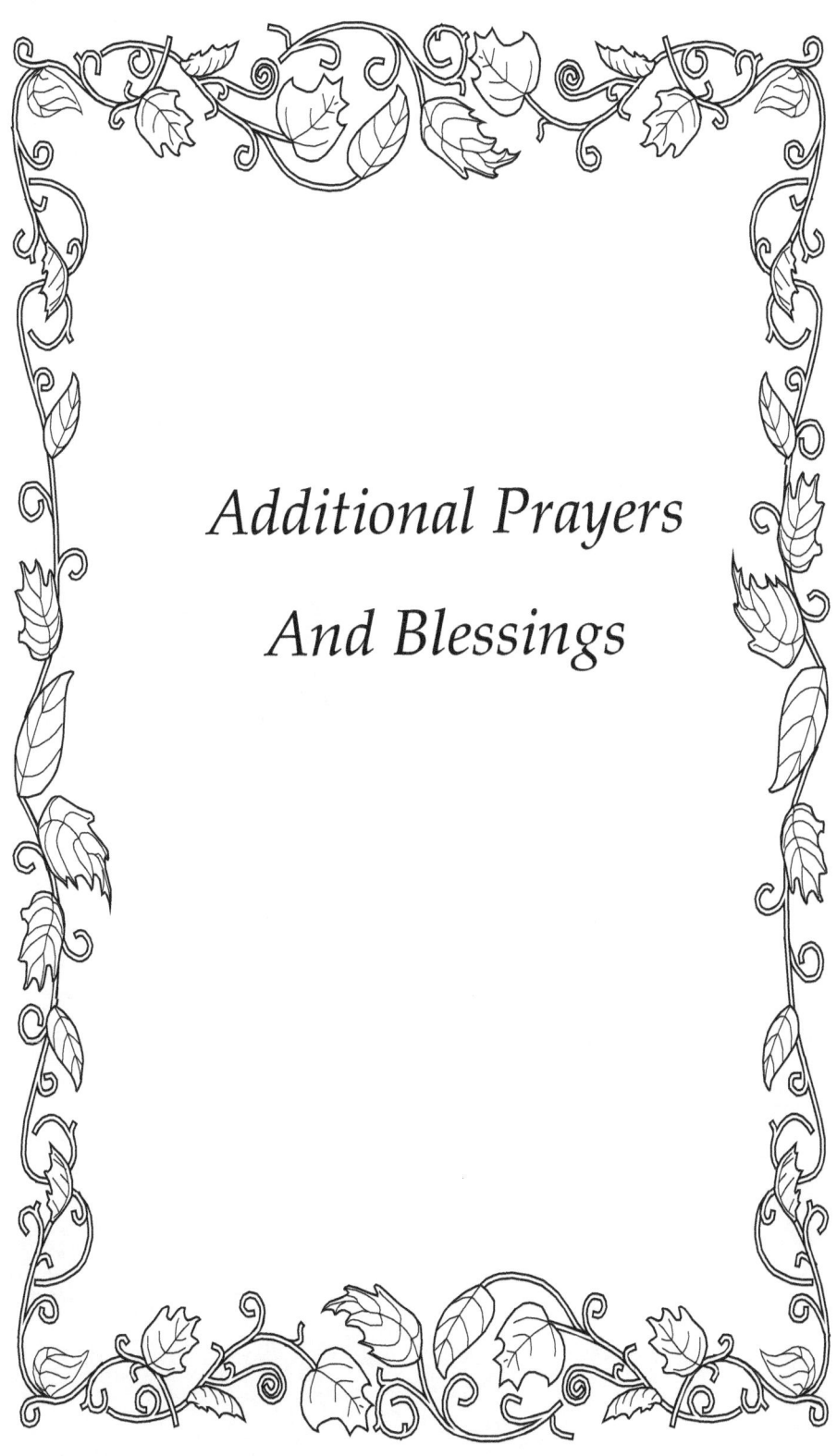

*Additional Prayers*

*And Blessings*

*May it be Your will O LORD our God, King of the Universe, to lead us and to direct our steps in peace, to guide us in peace, to support us in peace, and to bring us to our destination in life…*

# *Additional Prayers and Blessings*

༺༻༺༻༺༻༺༻༺༻༺༻༺༻༺༻༺༻

## Blessings for Torah Study

### Before study

Blessed are You, LORD our God, King of the Universe, Who has chosen Israel from all the peoples and given to them Your Torah on Mount Sinai to be a Light unto the Nations so that everyone would know how to serve You, our God, Creator of all things and by so doing merit everlasting life.

### After study

Blessed are You, LORD our God, King of the Universe, Who has chosen Israel to teach us Your Torah and to plant everlasting life in our midst, that we may be Your worthy servants, fashioned truly to Your Image, doing our duty according to Your will.

## Maimonides 13 Principles of Faith

I hereby declare my faith in GOD by affirming that:

1. I believe with perfect faith that GOD is the Creator and Ruler of all things. He alone has made, does make, and will make all things.

2. I believe with perfect faith that GOD is One. There is no unity that is in any way like His. He alone is our God; He was, He is, and He will be.

3. I believe with perfect faith that GOD does not have a body. Physical concepts do not apply to Him. There is nothing whatsoever that resembles Him at all.

4. I believe with perfect faith that GOD is first and last.

5. I believe with perfect faith that it is only proper to pray to GOD. One may not pray to anyone or anything else.

6. I believe with perfect faith that all the words of the prophets are true.

7. I believe with perfect faith that the prophecy of Moses is absolutely true. He was the chief of all prophets, both before and after him.

8. I believe with perfect faith that the entire Torah that we now have is that which was given to Moses.

9. I believe with perfect faith that this Torah will not be changed, and that there will never be another given by GOD.

10. I believe with perfect faith that GOD knows all of man's deeds and thoughts. It is thus written (Psalm 33:15), "He has molded every heart together, He understands what each one does."

11. I believe with perfect faith that GOD rewards those who keep His commandments, and punishes those who transgress Him.

12. I believe with perfect faith in the coming of the Messiah. However long it takes, I will await his coming every day.

13. I believe with perfect faith that the dead will be brought back to life when GOD wills it to happen.

**Morning Prayer**

*By Chris Bell*

Almighty GOD, Creator of all things, I thank You for returning my soul to my body and allowing me to see the beautiful day which You have created.

I thank You for watching over my family and keeping them away from all evil while we slept.

I thank You for everything which You have blessed me with today. I thank You for *[....food, clothing, medication, family, house, car, health, education, animals (pets), work, and etc]*.

Please forgive me for any sins which I have committed *(intentional/unintentional)*, I am sorry and will not do them again.

Please guide me and keep me away from all evil. LORD, please help me with *[whatever you need help with]*.

LORD, bless all the Jewish and Noahide people around the world.

LORD, please bless the countries of Israel and *(your country)*. May these governments know and acknowledge You and abandon all forms of corruption of any kind.

LORD, may You grant that whatever work I do, either at home or at work, be done safely and successfully.

**Naming a Child**

*By Reb Yirmeyahu Bindman*

*The father says before at least one male witness:*

He Who blessed our righteous forefather Noah that he should be fruitful and multiply, Who has now in His goodness blessed us with this child, may He bless *[him/her]* through the name which we give *[him/her]* here today.'

As *[he/she]* was born, so may *[he/she]* grow and marry and have children in *[his/her]* turn, to know Your truth and to walk in Your ways, for so we are commanded.

Therefore let us bear witness before You that *[his/her]* name shall be *[child's full name]*, to be known by this name for marriage, and for all *[his/her]* dealings according to Your Seven Holy Laws.

May it be Your will that under this name *[he/she]* shall have a good name, for life, for truth and for peace.

*State the child's full name.*

## Blessing a Child

*The father places his right hand on the child's head.*

May you be blessed of the Most High God, Maker of heaven and earth, to walk with Him among the Righteous of the Nations, now and for evermore.

*Additional Prayers and Blessings*

## Prayers for Places of Idolatry

Blessed are You, O LORD Our God, King of the Universe Who is long-suffering with those who transgress Your will.

## Prayer for Places Where Idolatry has been Uprooted:

Blessed are You, O LORD our God, King of the Universe Who has uprooted idolatry from *["Your holy land" if praying in Israel; "this place" if praying outside of Israel]*.

Just as You have uprooted idolatry from this place so too may You uproot it from all places and return the hearts of idolaters to the worship of You alone.

*Translated by Rabbi Saul Zucker from: The RAMBAM's* **Mishneh Torah, Laws of Blessings** *chapter 10, law 9 (quoting from the Talmud Bavli; Berakhot 54a and 57b.)*

## Blessing Before or After a Meal

Blessed are You, LORD our God, King of the Universe, Who feeds the whole world with His goodness, pleasantness, grace and mercy.

Due to His great goodness, we have never lacked and will never be in need of food forever.

His great Name feeds and gives everyone his livelihood, does good to everyone, and prepares food for all those that He has created.

## Various Blessings for Food

Blessed are You, LORD our God, King of the Universe, Who *(finish with appropriate ending below)*

### Wine

Creates the fruit of the vine.

### Bread

Brings forth bread from the ground.

## For mixtures of different kinds of food in one meal

Creates various kinds of food.

## Grain

Creates the fruit of the ground.

## Tree grown fruit

Creates the fruit of the tree.

## Earth grown fruit or vegetables

Creates the fruit of the ground.

# Blessings for Various Events

## When witnessing shooting stars, storms, thunderclaps, lightning and earthquakes:

Blessed be He whose strength and might fill the world.

### For rain and for good tidings

Blessed be He that is good and bestows good to all.

### For bad tidings or news of a death

Blessed be the True Judge.

### When seeing a rainbow

Remembers the Covenant, is faithful to His Covenant, and keeps His promises.

### Prayer for Travelers

*This is a prayer that can be said on the first day of travel after leaving your home or city, outside the city limits, and can be repeated every day until home again.* (Adapted from *Siddur Tehillat Hashem*, copyright 1978; pg. 86.)

May it be Your will LORD our God, King of the Universe, to lead us and to direct our steps in peace, to guide us in peace, to support us in peace, and to bring us to our destination in life, joy, and peace

## When returning add

and return *[me/us]* in peace.

## Continue

Deliver us from the hands of every enemy and lurking foe, from robbers and wild beasts on the journey, and from all kinds of calamities that may come to and afflict the world; and bestow blessing upon our actions.

Grant *[me/us]* grace, kindness, and mercy in Your eyes and in the eyes of all who behold us, and bestow bountiful kindness upon us.

Hear the voice of *[my/our]* prayer, for You hear everyone's prayer.

Blessed are You LORD, Who hears prayer.

## Prayer of Remembrance

> *Adapted by Rabbi Michael Katz from the Rosh Hashanah service.*

LORD, our God, You remember the deeds of the World and You consider all the creatures fashioned since earliest times.

All secrets and mysteries are revealed before You, for there is no forgetfulness before Your Throne of Glory and nothing is hidden from before Your eyes.

Everything is revealed and known before You, LORD our God, who observes all and sees to the very end of time.

You made it known from the beginning of creation that You would sit in Judgment over all that You create.

And even regarding countries, You decide which is destined for the sword and which for peace, which for hunger and which for abundance; and You consider all of Your creatures to remember them for life or death.

## Additional Prayers and Blessings

Who is not recalled before Your Divine Court? The remembrance of everything fashioned comes before You: everyone's thoughts, schemes and deeds, the accomplishments of man's activity, and even the motives behind man's deeds.

Fortunate is the man who does not forget You, and the human being who takes strength in You, for those who seek You, will never stumble nor will those who take refuge in You ever be humiliated.

For the remembrance of all Your works comes before You and You analyze the deeds of them all.

Indeed, You remembered Noah with love and in mercy You recalled his deeds, when You brought the waters of the Flood to destroy all living flesh because of their evil ways.

Consequently, his remembrance comes before You, LORD our God, to make his offspring as abundant as the dust of the world and his descendants like the sand by the sea; As it is written in Your Torah: "GOD remembered

Noah and all the beasts and all the cattle that were with him in the ark, and GOD caused a spirit to pass over the earth and the water subsided."

Therefore, LORD our God, we know that our eyes and hearts must be turned towards You alone to hope that our salvation and redemption will be justified in Your sight.

Judge us, then, in mercy as You judged Noah.

Judge us with compassion and send Your Messiah to Your chosen People, Israel, in order that we, the Righteous Gentiles, may also benefit from Your glory.

## On Passing

Almighty GOD, Who brought forth all mankind from the First Man, Who breathed into him the breath of life, and formed his body from the dust of all the earth so that it would accept him back wherever he might go, We now commit to the earth the body of our beloved friend *[state the name]* whose soul has passed to its eternal rest.

May *[he/she]* be bound up with You in the World to Come, and merit to the reward of the Righteous of all Nations, to behold Your truth as it is written in Your Seven Holy Laws.

As we are born into the world, so we must endure its trials and temptations, and thereby merit to that reward, for at the time of passing we take with us only good deeds and knowledge of the Torah.

So may it be with us all, in the blessing of Your endless mercy, for we and all that we have are Yours alone.

*Here ends Additional Prayers and Blessings*

*Personal Notes*

*Additional Prayers and Blessings*

*Service From the Heart*

*Readings From*

*The Psalms*

*... I will sing of Your power; yes, I will sing aloud of Your mercy in the morning: for You have been my defense and refuge in the day of my trouble.*

*Psalm 59:16*

# Readings From the Psalms

*With thanks to:*
*Frances Marakova, Reuven Ginat and Rabbi Tuvia Bolton*

| \multicolumn{6}{c}{The Daily Psalms – 30 day Reading} |||||| 
|---|---|---|---|---|---|
| Day | Psalm | Day | Psalm | Day | Psalm |
| 1 | 1-9 | 11 | 60-65 | 21 | 104-105 |
| 2 | 10-17 | 12 | 66-68 | 22 | 106-107 |
| 3 | 18-22 | 13 | 69-71 | 23 | 108-112 |
| 4 | 23-29 | 14 | 72-76 | 24 | 113-118 |
| 5 | 30-34 | 15 | 77-78 | 25 | 119: 1-96 |
| 6 | 35-38 | 16 | 79-82 | 26 | 119: 97- end |
| 7 | 39-43 | 17 | 83-87 | 27 | 120-134 |
| 8 | 44-48 | 18 | 88-89 | 28 | 135-139 |
| 9 | 49-54 | 19 | 90-96 | 29 | 140-144 |
| 10 | 55-59 | 20 | 97-103 | 30 | 145-150 |

## Psalms for Special Circumstances

| Circumstance | Psalm(s) to Read |
|---|---|
| **Prayer of Thanksgiving** | 107 or 136 |
| **Safety of Israel** | 83, 130, 142 |
| **Personal Safety** | 20 |
| **Illness** | 103 |
| **Recovery from Illness** | 6, 30, 41, 88, 103 |
| **The Seventh Day** | 92 and 104 |
| **On the Wedding Day** | 19 |
| **Giving Birth** | 20 |
| **Repentance** | 51 and 90 |
| **Peace** | 46 |
| **To Strengthen Belief** | 121 |
| **For Guidance** | 139 |
| **Rosh Chodesh (New Moon)** | 104 |
| Gratitude | 96, 116, 138, 136 |
| **Help with Troubles** | 23, 25, 26, 38, 54, 86, 102, 142 |
| Traveling | 91 |

| Circumstance | Psalm(s) to Read |
|---|---|
| **Happiness** | 1, 24, 33, 34 |
| **Mourning** | 16, 23, 40, 139 |

*Additional Readings*

*Service From the Heart*

# Wedding Ceremony

*When a man and a woman come together in harmony and purity, when they are devoted to one another in the shared responsibility of carrying out the duties prescribed for them by GOD and His teachings, they jointly become a resting place on earth for GOD's majesty.*

*Talmud, Sotah 17a*

# Wedding Ceremony

## A Few Customs

While not required of B'nai Noah, there is much beauty and wisdom in Jewish ceremonies.

Two of these ancient traditions of the Jewish people are called Badeken and the Chupah.

### Badeken

*The Veiling of the Bride by the Groom*

The veil symbolizes the idea of modesty and conveys the lesson that, however attractive physical appearances may be, the soul and character are paramount.

The chatan (groom) accompanied by family and friends, proceeds to the kallah's (bride's) room and places the veil over her face.

This is an ancient custom and serves as the first of many actions by which the groom signals his commitment to clothe and protect his wife.

It is reminiscent of Rebecca covering her face before marrying Isaac.

### Chupah

The wedding ceremony takes place under the *chupah* (canopy), a symbol of the home to be built and shared by the couple. It is open on all sides, just as Abraham and Sarah had their tent open on all sides to welcome friends and relatives in unconditional hospitality.

The *chupah* is usually held outside, under the stars, as a sign of the blessing given by GOD to the patriarch Abraham, that his children shall be as the stars of the heavens. (*www.aish.com/literacy/lifecycle/Guide_to_the_Jewish _Wedding.asp* Used with permission.)

## The Wedding Ceremony

**Leader:**

The LORD our God said "It is not good for man to be alone; I will make a fitting companion for him." So He cast a deep sleep upon the man, and while he slept, He took a part of the man and fashioned it into a woman and brought her to the man.

The man said "This at last is bone of my bone and flesh of my flesh." For this reason a man leaves his father and mother and clings to his wife, so they become one flesh. (Genesis 2:18, 21-24)

Thus, "When a man and a woman come together in harmony and purity, when they are devoted to one another in the shared responsibility of carrying out the duties prescribed for them by GOD and His teachings, they jointly become a resting place on earth for GOD's majesty." (Talmud, Sotah 17a)

**Witnesses:**

Blessed are You, LORD our King, Creator of the Universe Who has created mankind in Your image.

May Your blessings be upon *[Groom]*, son of *[Parents of Groom]* and upon *[Bride]* daughter of *[Parents of Bride]*, in accordance with Your Holy Word.

*The Bride and Groom then repeat the Marriage promise of commitment to each other.*

I promise to share with you in times of joy as in times of trouble, to talk and to listen, to respect and to appreciate you, to share my hopes, thoughts, and dreams with you, to raise our children in accordance with GOD's teachings, to treasure the unique person you are, and to always try to be sensitive to your needs.

Together, let us create a home that expresses our individuality and our love for one another, and may our home be filled with love, peace, happiness, and prosperity.

## The Exchange of Rings

**Leader:**

As a ring is a circle without end, it symbolizes your life-long commitment to each other before GOD and mankind.

**Witnesses:**

May the blessings and joy of *[Groom]* and *[Bride]* be without end.

**Leader:**

The ring also symbolizes one of the links in the eternal chain, for as GOD told Noah, "Go forth and multiply and replenish the earth."

**Witnesses:**

May you *[Groom]* and *[Bride]* and the children whom GOD may bless you with, link up to His eternal plan.

**Leader to the Groom:**

*[Groom]*, Do you give this ring as a token of your devotion to *[Bride]*?

*Groom responds.*

**Leader:**

*[Bride]*, do you receive this ring as a token of *[Groom's]*, devotion to you?

*Bride responds.*

**Leader:**

*[Bride]*, do you give this ring as a token of your devotion to *[Groom]*?

*Bride responds.*

*[Groom]*, do you receive this ring as a token of *[Bride's]* devotion to you?

*Groom responds.*

**Witnesses:**

Blessed are You, LORD our God, King of the Universe, Who creates joy, gladness, pleasure, delight, love, contentment, peace, and companionship, and bestows them upon the Bride and Groom.

**The Blessings**

**Leader:**

The fruit of the vine is associated with joy and happiness. In order to produce the wine, the fruit must be crushed together, each contributing to each other.

The same thing happens with marriage.

The bride and groom open themselves to each other and become a family, and each becomes part of the other's family.

We must all share and contribute and strive to make this world the place that GOD desires.

**All present say together:**

Blessed are You, LORD our God, King of the Universe, Who has created all things for Your glory.

Blessed are You, LORD our God, King of the Universe, Who has created mankind.

Blessed are You, LORD our God, King of the Universe, Who created man and woman in Your image, fashioning woman from man as his mate, that together they might perpetuate life.

Blessed are You, LORD, Who grants joy to the Bride and Groom.

**Leader:**

Blessed are You, LORD our God, King of the Universe Who creates the fruit of the vine.

*The Bride and Groom then drink from the cup of wine. The empty wine glass is then wrapped in a cloth and is stepped on and crushed by the groom. This symbolizes the destruction of the Temple and dates back to Talmudic times.*

*It represents our identifying with the Jewish people and the sorrow of the exile and recalls those, both Jew and non-Jew, who do not have the freedom to celebrate either religiously or publicly.*

**Leader:**

Even in this time of joy we are reminded that our lives are not complete.

We cannot experience ultimate joy until we live in the presence of GOD in His Kingdom.

**Parents of Bride and Groom or Leader says:**

With the blessings of GOD, the Creator of the Universe, and all those present, *[we/I]* now pronounce you husband and wife.

*The couple turns to leave the wedding canopy.*

**Witnesses say:**

LORD, grant perfect joy to these loving companions Mr. and Mrs. *[Groom's full name]*, as you did in the Garden of Eden to the first man and woman.

*Proceed to the Festive Meal*

*Personal Notes*

## Wedding Ceremony

*Service From the Heart*

*Funeral Service*

*O compassionate GOD Who dwells on high, grant perfect rest beneath the sheltering wings of Your Presence (Shechina), among the holy and pure whose souls shine as the brightness of the firmament.*

# Funeral Service

## Introduction

There is clearly an obligation to bury the deceased.

We find that Isaac and Ishmael buried their father, Abraham. Esau and Jacob, in turn, buried their father Isaac.

The Midrash tells us that it was in the merit of Japheth having joined Shem in the covering of Noah's nakedness, that the dead of Gog and Magog (nations descended from Japheth) merited burial. (Ezekiel 39)

Interment means burial in the ground, rather than in a tomb. Coffins are acceptable if made of wood.

The dead body is to be treated with respect; therefore viewing of the remains is not encouraged — the soul of the departed experiences agony that it's former host is seen in an impure state. For the same reason cremation is discouraged (a person should not be cremated unless he or she has specifically requested it). (Amos 2:1)

Funerals are not an appropriate occasion for ostentation, the simpler the better.

## The Service

*The coffin is placed to the side of the open grave or on the device designed to hold it above the grave.*

**The director of the service leads the mourners in prayer in unison:**

O LORD, what significance has man that You should consider him? Man is like a brief breath, a passing shadow; like grass which flourishes in the morning and in the evening fades and withers.

The years of our lives are threescore and ten or, with strength, fourscore; yet they are filled with toil and trouble, they are soon gone and we depart this world.

So teach us, O GOD, to use our days wisely. Guard the man who is blameless and behold he who is upright, for there is a future for the man of peace.

Surely the LORD will redeem my soul from the grave, He will surely receive me.

The LORD redeems the souls of His servants; none of those who take refuge in Him will be condemned.

The dust returns to the earth as it was, but the spirit returns to GOD Who gave it.

**The director says:**

The Sheltering Rock, His work is perfect, for all His ways are rooted in justice.

Our LORD is a God of faithfulness without iniquity; He is just and perfect in all His deeds.

He rules above and below, He takes away life and He gives it, He brings down to the grave and raises up from the grave.

*Eulogies are now given by those who knew the deceased and wish to share their memories.*

*It is good to reflect on the contribution the deceased made in his/her lifetime to the betterment of the world. It is appropriate to use the occasion to draw lessons from the life of the deceased for the improvement of his/her family and friends. The soul of the deceased will benefit from good deeds performed by those who were inspired by him/her.*

**All recite in unison:**

### Psalm 23

The LORD *is* my shepherd; I shall not want.

He makes me to lie down in green pastures: He leads me beside the still waters.

He restores my soul: He leads me in the paths of righteousness for His name's sake.

Yes, though I walk through the valley of the shadow of death, I will fear no evil: for You *are* with me; Your rod and Your staff they comfort me.

You prepare a table before me in the presence of my enemies: You anoint my head with oil; my cup runs over.

Surely goodness and mercy shall follow me all the days of my life: and I will dwell in the house of the LORD forever.

*The coffin is lowered into the grave and earth is shoveled into the grave by the mourners; enough to cover the coffin.*

**The director recites:**

O compassionate GOD, Who dwells on high, grant perfect rest beneath the sheltering wings of Your Presence (Shechina), among the holy and pure whose souls shine as the brightness of the firmament, to the soul of *[Deceased]*, *[son/daughter]* of *[Father of Deceased]* and *[Mother of Deceased]* who has gone to eternal rest and in whose memory charity is offered.

May *[his/her]* repose be in paradise.

May the Lord of Mercy protect *[him/her]* under the cover of His sheltering presence forever, and may *[his/her]* soul be bound up in the bond of eternal life.

May the LORD be *[his/her]* possession, and may *[he/she]* repose in peace and let us say, "Amen."

**The mourners reply:**

Amen.

**The chief mourners (closest relatives) say:**

The LORD gave and the LORD has taken away, praised be the Name of the LORD.

**Those gathered turn to the chief mourners and say to them:**

May the LORD, blessed be His Name, comfort you among the mourners of Zion and Jerusalem.

**The director leads the assembled in the reading of:**

**Psalm 16**

King David sang:

Protect me, GOD, for I have turned to You for shelter.

My soul declares that only the LORD is my God even though I am undeserving of His good.

It is only in the merit of my holy ancestors who are now in their graves that I enjoy Your favor.

Whereas those who run after pagan gods will see their sorrows multiplied; as for me, I will neither serve them nor allow their names to be on my lips.

The LORD is the source of my sustenance and it is He Who guides my destiny.

My role in GOD's plan is pleasant and all that befalls me is beautiful to me.

I will bless the LORD Who has given me good advice, even my own intellect steers me to choose His ways.

I have set the LORD before me at all times; because He supports me I shall not stumble.

Therefore, my heart rejoices and my soul is elated, even my physical body rests securely.

For You will not abandon my soul to the grave, You will not let Your pious one see destruction.

You will make known to me the ways that lead to eternal life, the full measure of joy in the light of Your countenance, the delights that are in Your power to bestow for eternity.

*Translated by Rabbi Michael Katz*

*Personal Notes*

## Service From the Heart

# Appendix

*And I, behold, I establish My covenant with you, and with your seed after you;*

*And God said, This is the token of the covenant which I make between Me and you and every living creature that is with you, for perpetual generations:*

*I do set My bow in the cloud, and it shall be for a token of a covenant between Me and the earth.*

*Genesis 9:9, 12-13*

# The Seven Noahide Laws Revealed in Genesis

By Frances Makarova

Reprinted from her website with permission.

The Seven Noahide Laws are found in the book of Genesis, but they are found in their transgression, not as specific commandments. In other words when one of these laws was transgressed, a comment is made in Genesis that a sin had been committed. (All references are from the Jewish text.)

1. **Idolatry**

Gen. 31:19-36 Rachel stole the **images** (idols) of her father, Laban.

Gen. 31:19 reads, "Laban had gone to shear his sheep, and Rachel stole the *teraphim* that belonged to her father."

The Commentary in the Stone Edition Chumash says about Gen. 31:19,

**"And Rachel stole the Teraphim that belonged to her father". The Teraphim were idols,** and Rachel took them to keep Laban from idol worship (Rashi). The Torah records this episode because her intentions were noble. (Midrash) Ramban derives the word from the root rapha, weak [see *Exodus* 5.17], alluding to the "weakness" of their prognostications. The *Zohar* relates the word to 'trph' and 'tvrph', denoting obscenity. Many consider them to have been household gods, supposed to be the protectors of the home, similar to the later Roman Penates, which were consulted as oracle {*R' Hirsch*}.

2. **Blasphemy**

Gen. 3:1-4 The Serpent falsely accused GOD.

Gen. 3:1-4 reads, "Now the Serpent was cunning beyond any beast of the field that the LORD GOD had made. He said to the woman, 'Did, perhaps, God say: "You shall not eat of **any tree** of the garden?"'"

The Serpent lied, and misrepresented what God really said. The serpent was falsely attributing to GOD that He had denied man access to "any tree," when, in fact, only a single specific tree was forbidden. In fact, man was permitted to eat of every tree except one.

> 16 And GOD commanded man saying, "Of **every tree** of the garden **you may freely eat:** 17 but the Tree of Knowledge of Good and Bad, you must not eat thereof; for on the day you eat of it, you shall surely die." (*Gen. 2:16*)

"The prohibition against blasphemy comes to teach us not to speak evilly against GOD, nor to detract from His exaltedness in any way by intentionally using words to lessen the reverence and faith befitting Him." (*Path of the Righteous Gentile* by Clorfene and Rogalsky)

3. **Murder**

Gen. 4:8-10-16, Gen. 6, Gen. 9:6 "Cain spoke with his brother Abel, and it happened when they were in the field, that **Cain rose up against his brother Abel** and **killed him.**"

One of the reasons that the flood was sent was because of theft, violence, murder and idolatry was common to all mankind (*Gen.* 6:11-12).

The Commentary in the Stone Edition Chumash says,

> Such is the progression of sin. It begins in private, when people still have a sense of right and wrong. But once people develop the habit of sinning, they gradually lose their shame, and immoral behaviour becomes the accepted - even required - norm. In Noah's time, the immoral sexual conduct of the people extended to animals, as well, until they too cohabited with other species.

Gen. 9:5-6 reads, "but of man, of every man for that of his brother I will demand the soul of man. 6) Whoever sheds the blood of man, by man shall his blood be shed; for in the image of God He made man."

## 4. Theft

Gen. 2:16 "And GOD commanded man saying, 'of **every tree** of the garden **you may freely eat:** 17 but **the Tree of Knowledge of Good and Bad, you must not eat thereof;** for on the day you eat of it, you shall surely die.'"

Gen. 3:6 "And the woman perceived that the tree was good for eating and that it was a delight to the eyes, and that the tree was desirable as a means to wisdom, and she **took** of its fruit and ate."

This was in direct disobedience of the command of GOD to not eat the fruit of that particular tree.

Gen. 31:19 "Laban had gone to shear his sheep, and Rachel **stole** the Teraphim that belonged to her father."

## 5. Forbidden Sexual Relationships

### Adultery

Gen. 20: 3 Abimelech knew **adultery** was a sin.

"And GOD came to Abimilech in a dream by night and said to him, '**Behold you are to die because of the woman you have taken; moreover she is a married woman.**'"

### Homosexuality

Gen. 19:5-7 "And they called to Lot and said to him, 'Where are the men who came to you tonight? Bring them out to us **that we may '*know*' them**.' 6) Lot went out to them to the entrance, and shut the door behind him. 7) And he said, 'I beg you, my brothers, do not act wickedly.'"

The context here clearly shows that the men of Sodom wished to have sexual relations with the two men (angels). And Lot indicated that he understood their intentions, because he then showed how Sodom had rubbed off on him, by offering the men his own virgin daughters.

## 6. Eating the Limb of a Living Animal

Gen.9:4-5 "**But flesh; with its soul its blood you shall not eat.** 5) However, your blood which belongs to your souls I will demand, of every beast will I demand it."

## 7. Establishing Courts of Justice

Gen.19:1-9. (The Gates of a city were where Judges sat to convene Courts of Justice.) Ruth 4: 1-11.

Gen. 19:1, 9 "The Two angels came to Sodom in the evening and Lot was sitting **at the gate of Sodom.** ...... 9) And they said, 'Stand back!' Then they said, '**This fellow came to sojourn and would act as a Judge?** Now we will treat you worse than them!' "

*Personal Notes*

# Brief History of B'nai Noah

By Larry Rogers

*Isaiah 56:7*

I will bring them to My holy mountain, and make them rejoice in the house of My prayer, [For My house is a house of prayer for all nations].

(Translation by Rabbi Aryeh Kaplan, *Eye of the Universe*)

These are the generations from Adam to Noah as recorded in Genesis 5:

Adam begot Seth

Seth begot Enosh

Enosh begot Kenan

Kenan begot Mahalalel

Mahalalel begot Jared

Jared begot Enoch

Enoch begot Methuselah

Methuselah begot Lamech

*Service From the Heart*

## Lamech begot Noah

Everyone knows the stories of Adam and Eve, of Cain and Abel, and of the Garden of Eden. We have heard the story of the serpent, and of the sins which forced mankind from the Garden and into a form of exile, which also brought death to the world. We have also heard the story of Noah and of the Ark, and how both Adam and Noah were considered to be good. In order to understand what happened between the time of Adam and the time of Noah, we need to go back and look at the events during the generations between them.

From the time that Adam and Eve went from the Garden, the growth of sin and injustice so corrupted mankind that GOD decided correction was not only necessary in their physical world but also in their spiritual world. This brought about the flood and the end of days for the children of Adam (B'nai Adam), with the exception of Noah and his family on the Ark. Because Noah in his time was considered by GOD to be a righteous man, Noah and his family were saved and mankind from the time of Noah was given a new name, children of Noah, (B'nai Noah).

This name lasted until the time of Abraham, Isaac, and Jacob when their descendants became the children of Israel (B'nai Israel). It was during the time of Abraham that the remainder of mankind decided to build a tower reaching to heaven itself in the city of Bavel, also called Babylon. Once again mankind was rebelling against GOD, who made a covenant with Noah and all of the Earth to never destroy it (and all mankind with it) again by way of the flood. By rejecting GOD, mankind reverted back to their former name: B'nai Adam. (See the story of the tower of Bavel in Genesis 11)

It is important to note that after the incident of the tower of Bavel, Abraham studied under Shem and Eber (at their academy) and that Shem was the Priest Malchizedek, King of (Jeru)Salem. It is also important to note that the Holy Language never departed from Shem, Eber, Abraham or his descendants. (for more information, see *The Seven Colors of the Rainbow* by Rabbi Yirmeyahu Bindman).

When Abraham made tithes to Malchizedek in Genesis 14:18-20, it is to Shem, that the tithes were offered, and the blessing from Malchizedek to Abraham is the transference of the high priesthood to Abraham. Abraham merited this transference due to his years of study at the academy, for his teaching the Seven Laws, and his acts of kindness. Abraham and Sarah continued teaching everyone they could about the Seven Laws and they were responsible for the spread of the laws around the world as others began learning and spreading the word.

These Seven Laws were the only mandatory laws for all mankind until the Exodus from Egypt of not only the Hebrew people, but the mixed multitude as well. When Moses came down the first time from the mountain and stated laws, they included the Seven Laws restated, along with the laws previously stated at Marah. (Exodus 19:1-9). These included the Seven Laws, civil laws, Sabbath laws, honor of parents, and for the Red Cow. When Moses went back up the mountain and received the 613 laws for the Hebrew people, he also received the Seven Laws for the nations, as well as the written Torah. (Exodus 24:3-4). (see commentary on Exodus 19 and 24 in *The Chumash, The Stone Edition*) Moses was also given the oral laws for both, which are mainly an explanation of what the laws comprise and directions for following them. It is through the oral laws and the Torah that Israel was designated as priests and teachers to the rest of the world. Israel was given the task of preserving and teaching these laws of GOD to all mankind.

Even in the times of the Temple, there were non-Jews who followed the Seven Laws as proscribed by GOD. Archeological findings of ancient Synagogue writings have mentioned GOD-fearers proving that there have been non-Jews in every generation who followed the teachings of the Seven Laws, who are seeking truth, and finding the correct path. Just as Noah and Abraham were considered righteous in their time, today there are those to whom we may look to for guidance from the Orthodox Jewish communities. Because the same teachings have been passed down through the ages, from generation to generation, Israel stands ready to teach non-Jews about the Seven Laws. In the mid to late 1980's, a spiritual reawakening began and we are seeing the fulfillment of the prophecies of Jeremiah 16:19-21, where the nations will come saying "we have inherited lies" and GOD will teach them, and Zechariah 8:23, which states "that ten men of every nation will take hold of the corner of the garment of every Jew, saying "Let us go with you, for we have heard that GOD is with you."".

Thanks in part to the internet and the abilities to record information, mankind can now receive the instructions from almost anywhere to almost anywhere. People now have the ability to discuss Torah in chat rooms, in forums, and through email. They can listen to recorded materials from rabbis in Israel or order books that have only been available in the country they were written in. The expansion of educational materials available to non-Jews about the Seven Laws and the practical application of them has enabled communities around the world to form and communicate with others.

*Personal Notes*

*Service From the Heart*

# Noahide Theology

By Rabbi Yechiel Sitzman

The Noahide Theology as the world oldest religious Faith dates all the way back to Adam. To understand this properly, one has to also consider the following:

**The Oral Tradition for Jews and Gentiles**

According to the simple Biblical narrative, the only commandments that GOD gave to Adam were to prohibit him from eating from the Tree of Knowledge and that he should have children. The Bible does not mention of any other laws given. The narrative continues with the story of Cain and Abel. When was the commandment not to murder given? Who told Cain that it was wrong to murder his brother? Prior to the flood, there was no written Biblical injunction of law. If not, how could GOD consider any human action to be bad and thus accountable for punishment? Without having knowledge of law and morality, how could the generation of the flood have known their actions to be evil before GOD?

Some might wish to say that everyone knows deep down the difference between right and wrong. But this is not always true. Different cultures hold different values. What one culture may hold as perfectly acceptable another culture might find repugnant. Modern logic claims that everyone knows the difference between basic right and wrong; and that even without the giving of such laws, the pre-flood generations should have known better, even without being told. While this logic might sound good to us today, it does not have any value by Biblical standards.

According to the *Bible*, (ref. *Lev.*), ignorance of the law lessens a violator's punishment, or exempts him entirely. Therefore, if punishment came, as we see with regards to the flood, then we can logically conclude that certain laws were given (and violated) even though the *Bible* does not out rightly record the giving of these laws. The holy Rabbis teach us a point that is essential for any student of the *Bible* to learn and to learn well. Not everything was written in the *Bible*.

As with every ancient culture, the nation of Israel held a very rich Oral Tradition that fills in many of the blanks in the Biblical narrative. Over the many years, the great majority of these Oral traditions have been written down and this is how we know of them today.

## Before the Flood

The Jewish Oral Tradition teaches us that indeed, Adam and all his descendents were commanded to observe certain universal commandments. Numbering only six, these universal laws were given to Adam so that his progeny (offspring) would learn how to create and establish a society based upon morality, righteousness and human rights. The six universal laws given to Adam are as follows:

1. No idolatry

2. No blasphemy

3. No murder

4. No sexual immorality

5. No theft

6. To establish just courts

Short, simple and direct to the point. It is these six principles that human society was originally commanded to observe. The *Bible* does not overtly record this, yet the *Bible* does record mankind being held accountable for them.

**After the flood**

God repeated these laws to Noah and all his children with the addition (Gen. 9:4) of the forbiddance of eating part of a living animal. None of these universal laws are recorded outright in the *Bible* as having been given before the flood. Even though GOD punishes Cain for murder and later destroys an entire generation for similar sins, nowhere is there recorded the giving of the laws that defined such actions as sin. The *Bible* does delete many important facts which, for reasons known only to GOD, He chose not to include. For example, where did Cain and later Seth and others find their wives? The *Bible* does not record their wives' births. Where did they come from?

The *Bible* also doesn't mention the names of any of the pre-flood matriarchs and mothers with the exception of Eve (and one or two other women). Are we to assume that the other fathers of old were born without mothers simply because the *Bible* doesn't mention any mothers? Obviously such type of thinking is quite insulting to human intelligence. We take it for granted that although certain things are not clearly mentioned they, nevertheless, are still there.

Jewish tradition and religion, since its Sinai foundations, have been built upon a two-fold type of knowledge. The first is the absolute written Word of GOD and the second, equally important and authoritative, the Oral Tradition that provided the comprehensive meaning and official interpretation of the written Word. Only with the proper combination of the two can the *Bible* ever be properly understood.

In addition, every human being is expected to follow principles of action that can be deduced by unadulterated common sense that is based upon the axioms evident from the above mentioned

Seven Laws. Examples of this are the obligations of giving charity to the poor and hospitality to travellers, as well as not displaying disrespect toward one's parents.

The chain of tradition of these universal laws was broken for most people. At the revelation at Mount Sinai it was revealed again to Moses. There were also some minor changes in some of the laws at that time. From then onward, all non-Jews are expected to observe these laws as they were given to Moses because they were revealed (a second time) to him. Throughout history there have been individuals who were committed to this way of life.

In recent years Noahides have begun to organize themselves into communities and have been establishing contact between them using modern communication methods.

Noahide theology is the same as the theology of Judaism. However, non-Jews are not required to accept all the details of this theology to the extent that Jews are. Observant Noahides are the Non-Jews in Judaism. Just as the Priests, Levites, women etc... have particular Laws given to them at Sinai, so do Noahides have particular Laws. Together we all make one True Universal Religion, walking in the Ways of our Creator.

And just as Noahides have the Seven Universal Laws to follow, they also must have an oral tradition that encapsulates how to observe them.

*Personal Notes*

# Noahide Commandments

From *Atem Adai*
By Rabbi Yoel Schwartz
Translated by Yitzhak A. Oked Sechter
Reviewed and corrected by Rabbi Yechiel Sitzman
in consultation with Rabbi Yoel Schwartz

(c) 2004 Rabbi Yoel Schwartz

಄಄಄಄಄಄಄಄಄

## Introduction

This work deals mainly with the effort of defining the commandments that the non-Jewish nations should fulfill or make an effort to do so. In addition to the seven basic commandments, there are several other active commandments that have not been clarified and explained in depth in the scriptures and subsequent Torah literature. Just the same, according to what is written in the Torah the Talmud and the Midrash, we are able to learn something from the actions of those that existed before the Torah was given to Israel. According to the Talmud (Yomah 28b), the Patriarchs, Abraham, Isaac, and Jacob upheld more commandments than what the children of Noah were called upon to do. Even commandments that the sages turned into laws many generations later were kept by the Patriarchs.

According to these same sources, Jacob already upheld all of the 613 commandments of Judaism. This is why Jacob's children are no longer called children of Noah but children of Israel. Just the same, we can learn from some of their actions and from their expectations from those that lived during their generation regarding the ways that any person who wants to come closer to GOD and attain spiritual fulfillment, should act.

The matters that we are trying to explain in this work are not in any way an effort to try and establish a new religion. It is rather an attempt to look at the Scriptures and other Torah literature and reach conclusions concerning what a person should do or try to do. Our prayers are that this modest beginning will bring others to write a complete book and that it should cover a greater scope. In order to help all those among the nations who are looking for ways to come closer to GOD.

Judaism forbids establishing a new religion, as explained by the Rambam (Kings 10, 5:6-9): "The principle of the matter: You cannot allow them to establish a new religion or to carry out commandments from this knowledge..." Anyway, what we are doing here in connection with the Children of Noah is not the establishment of a new religion. Since a foreigner (Gentile) is not ordered in writing to fulfill them, but only, if by his own free will, he wishes to carry out such commandments as the Rambam wrote: "We are not allowed to stop a child of Noah that seeks to be compensated by fulfilling the (some of those) laws of the Torah (that were only commanded to the Jews)." So it seems that the establishment of a new religion occurs only when a person comes and says that he has been ordered by GOD to fulfill such and such a law and not when he is trying to reach a degree of spiritual perfection by fulfilling the commandments that the children of Israel have been ordered to carry out.

# Foreword

### On The Importance of Doing (Fulfilling and Carrying Out)

"We will fulfill and we will hear" (Shabbat 88a).

Here we will try to explain the importance of spiritual fulfillment and its effect on the personality of the person. We will also see why it is not enough to feel this spiritual fulfillment in the heart, but that it must be accompanied by concrete actions. All this has been explained in the Torah and was understood as something quite simple by many intellectuals of the world like Soren Kirkgegard (In "A Jew, Who Is He, What Is He?" page 22) who said, "A belief that does not bring in its wake a fulfillment and a change, is a false one. The greatest believer, who carries out his belief with great enthusiasm, but shows no sign of a complete change in his life, proves that his belief is simply part of his own imagination only. The influence and recognition of a belief in a human being depends on the way he carries out his day-to-day life and manages to control and suppress his desires, stops doing evil and the actions he takes to carry this out."

The Greek philosophers, who did not believe in a practical religion, but believed that human perfection comes from recognizing and studying the truth, believed just the same, that a person must carry out and fulfill deeds that will teach him spiritual perfection: In his Kuzari, Rabbi Yehudah HaLevi thus wrote (Article A, Part A), "Question the truth on the things that you want to know, in order that your brain will act and not be acted upon. Talk to the point and in truthful ways. This will help you seek and recognize the truth. Then you will demand less, be more humble and accumulate good character traits."

The Philosophers did not recognize GOD or the need to act accordingly to His commandments. This is why they believed that human beings can act in any way suitable that will bring them to fulfillment of their goals. Just the same, these intellectuals understood that it was not enough for a person to acquire education and knowledge but that he also needed to carry out and act in order that his internal thinking could turn into a reality. Which is exactly what the Torah tells us to do, and we will bring several examples here.

A) The Precepts (Mitzvot) connected to prayers: These precepts connected to prayers are done through the heart as it is stated in Ta'anit 2, "and to labor for him with all your heart - what is the service of the heart - it is prayer." Anyway it is not enough to pray from the heart. If a person has some thoughts that stem from his heart but does not utter them out with his lips, then he has not fulfilled the commandment as it is stated in Berachot 20, "Thoughts are not the same as an utterance."

B) Repentance: The precepts connected to repentance are also connected to the heart: Nevertheless, "A person repenting must confess with his lips and say the things he has decided to do through his heart" (Rambam, Repentance, Chapter 2).

C) Ownership: When ownership is transferred, the most important part in this transaction is that the heart of the original owner agrees with the action. But all of this is not legal until some sort of action of transference is performed, such as that a deed or legal paper is signed or changes hands or the transfer of ownership done according to the Jewish religion (Halacha). (This includes an action that is accepted as a valid transference of ownership by the society where the transaction is taking place.)

D) Marriage: It is not enough for both sides to agree to marry and to live like a family, but a legal action must also be carried out for this agreement to be formal.

From all these examples we have learned that it is not enough for the heart to tell you to do something. There is a need for some sort of act to carry out the will of the heart. For this reason the spiritual fulfillment of a person is not reached unless it is carried out by action. The belief and the desire to be close to GOD and the actions connected with it must be according to the precepts (Mitzvot) that GOD set forth in the Torah.

There is, sometimes, an opposite process when outside actions (not connected or controlled by the person) influence the internal thinking of a person as it is explained in Sefer Ha'Chinuch #16, explaining why the Torah has so many practical precepts: "Know that a person is governed by his actions. His heart and all his thoughts are influenced by the actions that he is involved in be they good or bad. Even a wicked man whose thoughts are concentrated on doing evil all day, if he should start studying Torah and Mitzvot, even if he is not doing it for GOD's sake, he will start acting in a more positive manner. This is because the heart goes after the deeds. The same holds true, concerning a righteous man, who lives according to the Torah and Mitzvot, but makes a living from dubious transactions, or if for example he is forced by the King or ruler to deal in such dubious matters, he will eventually be transformed from a righteous man to an evil one."

In Mesilat Yesharim (Chapter 7), it is written, "Alacrity is brought about by the internal enthusiasm of a person. But even if a person lacks this internal enthusiasm, he should carry out and do things in an accelerated pace, this will bring about an internal enthusiasm. Since external actions brings about internal ones."

The Rambam, in his commentary to Avot, wrote, "If a person wants to give a certain sum to charity, it is worthwhile to divide this charity into several portions and give it away at different intervals and not at one time. By doing so, it has a greater effect on a person, than if he would give the sum to charity all at one time. This, despite the fact that to do so, he must invest more time and effort."

The actions of a person should be done in order to fulfill and carry out the commandments of the Creator, since these are the things that elevate a person. As the Maharal from Prague wrote in Tiferet Yisrael (Chapter 4), "The commandments of the Torah can be likened to a rope by which a person is drawn out of a hole or a well. The person is drawn from the lowest levels to the higher levels of the world. The more he does, the more he removes materialism from himself, which then enables him to sit next to the Lord of Hosts."

The meaning of the word Mitzvot in Hebrew comes from the root Unite and Bind. Which means that each mitzvah unites and binds the person to the Creator of the world (see Tanya). In Tanna d'bei Eliyahu (Chapter 9), it is written, "I testify before heaven and earth, Israel and the nations, man and woman between a servant and handmaiden, the Holy Spirit rests upon a person according to his actions."

The fulfillment of the commandments in the Torah, builds the character of a person and raises him to a level of perfection, as it is written in Deuteronomy 4:14, "And the LORD commanded me at that time to teach you statutes and ordinances, that *la'asot'chem* – you might do them..." [The Hebrew *la'asot'chem* also means "you shall make (i.e. build) yourselves."]

This word *la'asotchem* teaches us here that the statutes and ordinances, the mitzvot, build the person and it does not merely mean that a person must carry them out. This is why it is written in this special way. A person must be trained on the way he should build his life, starting from early childhood. Anyone reading books dealing with child-care can find many examples there. But even as a grownup, a person must take a grip on himself, if he wants to "discover himself" and find a real meaning to his life. The Noahide laws are logical. Many intelligent people will even agree that there is a need for them, but this is not enough. We must remember that we must carry out these ordinances and statutes because we have been ordered to do so by the Creator. They were given to Adam and Noah, then again given on Mount Sinai. Part of the Torah was given on Mount Sinai to the Israelites as a Holy Nation of Priests (Exodus 19:2). The remaining part is intended for entire human race. The Rambam wrote in Melachim-Kings (8:11),

> Every person that agrees to carry out the seven Mitzvot of the children of Noah, and does this in a careful manner, is a righteous gentile, and has part in the world to come, meaning that he carries this out

because God has ordered him to do so in the Torah, through Moses. But if these seven mitzvot are carried out just because he feels a necessity to do so, then he is not a Ger Toshav (Gentile resident in Israel), nor a righteous gentile or one of its sages.

The Mitzvot have been handed down to us in the form of an order, but just the same we are called to accept them gladly. A person must accept the Mitzvot with love. Despite the hardships in fulfilling them, he must carry them out. This also has an educational value.

A person who wants to do only those good deeds that he feels impelled to perform without being ordered to do so stresses his own importance. He thinks that he is the focus of everything. But when a person decides to carry out the Mitzvot because he has been ordered to by GOD, then he feels the importance of the GOD that orders. It is only then that he manages to discover and find all his hidden powers in order to carry out these mitzvot. These hidden powers cannot be tapped to their utmost if a person carries out the mitzvot simply because he has the sudden urge or mood to do so. This decision is strengthened even more when the person announces it before three learned and wise Jews. This act transforms the person into a Ger Toshav. Even today, when, since all of the Israelites have not yet returned to their land, the laws concerning a Ger Toshav are not applicable – in reference to the special privileges which would otherwise apply to a non-Jew who has made such a declaration – such a declaration made before three observant Jews nevertheless still enhances the status of the non-Jew.

This declaration should include: belief in the principles of the existence of the one true GOD, who is everlasting, the Creator of all things, guides all of his creations, is the One that gave the Torah on Sinai for all of humanity, and oversees all the actions of the human beings to reward and punish them for their deeds. Then the person should state that he is willing to fulfill the seven mitzvot that were given to Noah. (There are those who believe that this announcement should be accompanied by submersing in a pool of at least 660 liters of water, like the sea, spring or a man-made pool built in the earth. However we know of no basis for this view.)

## Commandments Dealing With Matters Between Man and GOD

**Introduction**

The basis of all commandments is the belief that GOD who is the creator of all things, and capable of doing everything, has commanded us to fulfill them. Habakkuk summed it up by stating that a righteous person shall live through his belief. Also in Chapter 9:23 of Jeremiah it is stated: "But let he who glories, glory in this, that he understands and knows Me, that I am the Lord who exercises loving kindness, judgment and righteousness in the world: for it is these things that I desire, says the LORD."

The Gaon, Rabbi Shmuel Ben Hafni, stated that the important commandment for the people of other nations is the belief that the LORD our God is the Creator and director of the world, that He is actively involved in the lives of every person and that He is One.

The Rambam writing to Rav Hasdai stated: "Quoting from our sages, the righteous people from other nations have a place in the world to come, if they have acquired what they should learn about the Creator."

In the category of the belief in the one true GOD, the seven commandments to the children of Noah include the prohibitions against worshiping other gods and against blasphemy (which includes professing atheism). There are, of course, many commandments connected with the belief in the one true GOD. They include:

(a) Loving GOD
(b) Praying to Him
(c) Thanking Him for His generosity
(d) Trusting Him
(e) Honoring Him
(f) Sanctifying His Holy Name
(g) Prohibiting the desecration of His Holy Name

(h) Moving away from those who do not believe in Him such as atheists, infidels and impious people

(i) Having a direct relationship with Him, not through any intermediaries. This is why it is forbidden to pray among others to any angels or to the dead or to any person past, present or future!

(a) Loving GOD: Inasmuch as the Israelites were commanded not only to love GOD, but that they should also teach all mankind to love GOD, we see that all people are supposed to love Him. One of the first to do so was Abraham the Patriarch (Sifri Vetchanan), and in the Sefer Mitzvot it says, "This mitzvah [loving GOD] includes that we should call every human being to believe in Him and worship only Him… See to it that you make Him beloved to your fellow men just as your forefather Abraham did."

(b) Praying to GOD: Noah was punished for not praying so that his fellow men might be saved from the flood. According to the sages (Zohar Leviticus p15b), this is the reason that the flood is named after Noah. However, the destruction of Sodom is another case. This event is not named after Abraham because he did pray to save the people of Sodom before it was destroyed. One type of prayer is a request by a human being to GOD. There is also a thanksgiving prayer that is an important obligation from a person for all the things for which he is thankful such as: his occupation that gives him a livelihood, health, family, etc. and especially if something good has occurred to him personally. This brings us to thanksgiving.

(c) Thanking GOD for His generosity: Again the best example is from Abraham. In the Gemara Sota:10, Abraham in Beersheva would invite people to eat and drink with him. At the end of the meal he would request from them that they should bless and thank GOD for his generosity.

(d) Trusting in GOD: Joseph was punished by two years being added to his stay in prison because he requested help in getting a prison release from Pharaoh's wine chief instead of putting his full trust in GOD (Genesis Rabbah 29:3).

(e) Honoring GOD: To honor one's father and one's mother is a threshold to honoring the heavenly Creator Father who begat us. One should honor and give credit to all wise Torah teachers and sages, especially those who teach you Torah. He who does not fully honor his Torah teachers dishonors GOD. A person must be very careful in fulfilling this commandment. To give honor to GOD, he must give honor to the Torah and to its wise teachers. Honoring GOD also extends to honoring all of GOD's creations because they are His creations. In particular one should honor elderly persons because these persons have most likely witnessed in their lifetime many instances of GOD'S intervention. Through my giving honor to them I am honoring someone who recognizes the greatness of the Creator.

The importance of fulfilling oaths and vows made in GOD's name can be understood in the framework of giving honor to GOD.

(f) To be willing to make every effort for the Sanctification of His Holy Name (i.e. to publicize His greatness and the importance of serving Him): There are opinions that in some situations, a non-Israelite is even called upon to die as a martyr to protect the honor of GOD (i.e. not to worship other gods). All agree that he must be willing to die rather than to commit murder. The person must know that everything occurring is according to the will of GOD and accept it without complaining against Him. This commandment is part of the previous one.

(g) Prohibition against desecrating GOD's name: This was one of the reasons that the people of Sodom were punished. In this respect a GOD-fearing person must be especially careful in the manner in which he conducts himself. If he does not act properly, others will point to him and say. "Look how unethically (or however badly) that person is acting and he is a believer in GOD." This constitutes a desecration of His name in an indirect way.

(h) Not Having Fellowship With Unbelievers and Impious People: Relations with unbelievers are only for the purpose already mentioned before. It is the duty of everyone to ensure that all human beings believe in the one true GOD and do His will. Consequently a person must be extremely careful that he does not bring another person to sin by his association with the ungodly. Psalm 1:1 says. "Happy is the man who has not walked/followed after the advice of wicked men, who has not stood/lingered on the path of immoral men, and who has not sat [or made his permanent dwelling] with scoffers." This is especially true when participating in religious services where the ritual or sermons, songs or prayers are violating the Torah.

**Walking in the Halacha**

Faith is *Emunah*, what you believe, while *Halacha* means how you walk or conduct yourself in practice of what you believe. We do the things we do because we are what we are. A man will practice what he believes. If he professes to believe in righteousness, but practices unrighteousness, he is a practical, practicing atheist. "Noah was a righteous man in his generation." "Noah walked with GOD." "Noah found grace in the eyes of GOD" (Genesis 5:8, 6:9).

**The Laws of Belief**

A. It is a commandment (mitzvah) for a human being to believe that there is a creator of the universe, that He is Eternal, the First and Last of everything. He is One, and there is no unity comparable to his or god outside Him. His unity cannot be multiplied or divided. He is exclusive in his unity, and there is no other like Him in the universe. There is none other or any other sources that have His power or His capability. All the sources of power and energy in the universe stem and come from Him.

B. It is a commandment for a human being to study his belief, and to observe the creation to see and to recognize His greatness. It is written in Isaiah chapter 40, "Lift up your eyes and see Who created these." Similarly he should study history to observe what has happened in time past and present: It is also commanded to observe what has happened in history to see how GOD has been in charge and the One who rules over all events. "Remember the days of old, consider the years of many generations. Ask thy father, and he will show thee; thy elders, and they will tell thee. When the Most High divided to the nations their inheritance, when he separated the sons of Adam, he set the bounds of the people according to the number of the children of Israel. For the LORD's portion is His people; Jacob is the lot of his inheritance" (Deuteronomy 32:7-9). "Remember the former things of old; for I am GOD, and there is none else; I am GOD and there is none like me, Declaring the end from the beginning, and from ancient times the things that are not yet done, saying, My counsel shall stand, and I will do all my pleasure" (Isaiah 46:10-11). Israel was created by GOD to receive the Torah and give the prophets to a pagan world that had many thousands of gods. Israel's unique prophetic character is different and separates Israel from all other nations. Israel is the only nation on earth whose entire history was written before it happened. The Jews' mission against a polytheistic world has had an unbelievable impact against polytheism. Even the atheists say, "There is no God." They do not say, "There are no gods."

C. It is appropriate to say aloud what you believe in order to strengthen the conviction in your heart. For example: There is one GOD and His name is One. (Zech.14:9). There can be no compromise on pronouncing aloud this belief. The Torah concept of GOD does not allow him to have a split personality. It is worthwhile to say different basic concepts of belief toward the one true GOD loudly and clearly, such as the affirmation (Shema Yisrael) "Hear O Israel..." Here are other sentences that are worthwhile repeating at regular intervals, since they are among the basics of belief:

- I believe with a complete belief that the Creator, blessed be His Name, He alone, created and made all the created things. He alone made, is making and will continue to make all things.

- He is One, and there is none other like Him, in no way or manner. He alone is our Lord in the past, present, and future.

- He does not have body. Nobody can be like Him, and no imagination can detail or describe Him. No picture can depict Him; no image can portray Him. No material can contain His essence. No wood, no stone, no plant, no star nor constellation can be compared to Him.

- GOD is first and last. Of no man can this be said.

- To GOD and GOD alone we should pray (meaning that no use at all of any mediator should be made in a prayer between man and GOD).

- GOD knows all the thoughts and actions of a person. He pays good wages to those who do good while punishing those who do evil. The most significant compensation will be in the next world (after death). There will also be worldwide compensation with the coming of the Messiah. After that, there will be a resurrection of the dead.

- GOD gave the Torah to the Jewish people so that they bring merit to all of humanity. This Torah has never changed and will never be changed. Part of this Torah was given to the whole human race. Another part of the Torah was given only to the Israelites. (Every human being can join and be part of Judaism by conversion, but a person is not obligated to do so.) If a person fulfills the commandments of a son or daughter of Noah, then that person will have a part in the world to come.

## The Prohibition Against Doing Anything that Contradicts the Belief in One GOD

(1) It is prohibited to worship any other god, in any form or matter at all. If a person is forced to do so, he should try as hard as possible not to carry out such a demand. If he is being threatened by death, there are those that believe that he should be willing to die as a martyr if he does so while being witnessed by ten Jews or ten people of other nations who worship only the One true GOD. A person is not allowed to give honor to other gods, to hug or kiss them; to swear by them, to pray to or worship them. He is not allowed to produce an idol so that others can worship it. He is not even allowed to produce it for artistic purposes. He is not allowed to participate in any rites connected with the worship of other gods even if this person is passive and does not take any active participation in it. All this is so that he will not be misunderstood and cause others to sin because of his action. It is the duty of a person to degrade and hold in contempt all other gods or any form of idolatry.

(2) To deny the existence of GOD is worse than worshipping other gods. Some maintain that this is included in the prohibition of worshipping other gods. Others maintain that it is considered blasphemy since there is no greater insult to the one true GOD than denying his existence.

(3) It is appropriate to refrain from the following because they too are considered related to the worship of other gods:

(a) Dealing in magical traits, such as predicting with the aid of a crystal ball, or hypnotizing yourself so that you can predict the future or dealing in black magic or trying to predict the future through other means such as horoscopes or things like that;

(b) Believing in superstitions, such as bad luck because of a black cat or good or bad luck connected to certain numbers;

(c) Gathering animals for magic, like hypnotizing them;

(d) Dealing in spiritualism;

(e) Trying to communicate with the dead.

## The Prohibition Against Insulting or Offending the Honor of GOD

1. The prohibition against cursing GOD by His name or by any other substitute for His name;

2. The prohibition against denouncing GOD or his Torah;

3. The prohibition against asking philosophical questions about what occurred before the creation of the world. We should only contemplate what has occurred since the creation (and not before). This is so that we can try to realize and grasp the greatness of the one true GOD as we have already previously mentioned;

4. It is prohibited to interbreed animals or plants that are not of the same species.

5. It is prohibited to take on or initiate a new religion. But Noahides, fulfilling the seven commandments (mitzvot), are not taking on a new religion since these seven commandments are mentioned in the Torah. Noahides may perform commandments that were given specifically to the Jews in the hope that they will be rewarded for them, provided that they don't consider these actions obligatory. It is also important to note that according to some opinions there are some commandments that Noahides should not fulfill because they are connected with holiness and given specifically to Israel. These are the commandments of Tefillin and mezuzah. All agree that the child of Noah should not observe the seventh day of the week, Saturday, as Shabbat, as given to Israel as a day of rest, but it is appropriate for him to inculcate the message of the Shabbat, as will be explained further on. It is important to study the laws of the Torah that apply to

Noahides. However they are prohibited from studying those parts of the Torah that don't apply to them. This refers mainly to the oral law (Talmud, Rambam etc.) but also when reading the Bible it is better to skip those laws that don't apply to them.

**Explanations**

According to Rabbinic literature, GOD does not want people to question matters connected with that which existed before the creation. As creatures in creation, we can only comprehend GOD in and through creation as Creator. "When I consider the heavens, the work of Your fingers, the moon and the stars, which You have ordained; [I think:] What is man that You are mindful of him" (Psalm 8:3). Only the Torah existed before creation. David declared in Psalm 119: "Your word, O GOD is from everlasting to everlasting." "With GOD's word the heavens were made, and all the heavenly hosts [were fashioned] with the breath of His mouth" (Psalm 33:6).

Genetic engineering is a delicate subject. There is room to postulate that engaging in some kinds of genetic engineering constitutes a violation of the prohibition to crossbreed. Since the prohibition of crossbreeding does not include hybrid breeding of plants and animals and breeding to develop a hybrid within a species of like kind the same can be said regarding some kinds of genetic engineering.

Even if it is permitted, those dealing in this field must be careful that through this work they will not feel that they are capable of divorcing themselves from GOD and His creation, that scientists will not feel that they are capable of creating independently from GOD, like Adam in his first sin.

## Commandments Concerning Honoring GOD

1. A PERSON MUST HONOR GOD AND HIS TORAH, including the sages, teachers of Torah, elderly persons, holy books, holy places like houses of prayer and cemeteries where tzadikim are buried. If a person makes a vow in GOD's name, he must fulfill his oath. If he does not make the vow in GOD's name but pledges to do something for someone else, he must fulfill it. It seems that if he made the oath to himself or concerning only himself it is also appropriate that he fulfill his vow. In doing so, he honors himself. A person who makes a vow to himself in the name of GOD is honoring GOD by fulfilling it. If a person makes a pledge to a fellow man, he must fulfill it since it is in the category of civil laws that are incumbent on Noahides. By not fulfilling pledges, vows, oaths and covenants, one dishonors GOD, Torah and himself.

2. Before performing any work, or whatever, it is suitable for a person to say that he will do this thing with GOD's help, in

order that he will remember that all of his successes are derived and come to him only through GOD.

3. A Noahide, to fulfill the seven commandments, should strive to learn carefully and seriously all his obligations concerning all the seven commandments of the children of Noah. If there is a problem, or if the person does not know exactly how to fulfill a certain obligation as a Noahide, he should turn to a Jewish Torah authority who is acquainted with the subject matter to make a decision on the issue or question. Any learned Jew can teach non-Jews only if he himself is a Torah observant Jew. He must believe that GOD gave Moses the written law and also the oral law. He must observe Shabbat and Kashrut and the other Mitzvot.

**Prayers**

Noahides are not commanded to have formal prayers. It should be left to the individual how, what, and when he will pray. Prayer is permitted, but not commanded. There are several types of prayers; requests, recognition of GOD's grandeur, thanksgiving to Him for good things that He has done for a person and strengthening one's faith, as it is stated in many places in the book of Psalms. It is advisable to turn toward the direction of Eretz Yisrael, Jerusalem and the Temple Mount when praying.

A Siddur for Bnei No'ach should be established for those who wish to have guidance in prayer. Below are some suggestions for formal prayer that might be included in a Bnei Noah Siddur:

1. Regular prayers might be said everyday that could include a statement saying, "Know today, and place it on your heart that GOD is the Lord in the heavens above and on the earth below -- there is nothing else." Also he might recite the affirmation, "Hear O Israel..."

2. Prayer in time of emergency or danger: A person who finds himself in danger should recite an appropriate chapter from the book of Psalms, for example, chapter 20. If the emergency is due to illness, chapter 103. If he needs to strengthen his belief in GOD so as to receive His help, chapter 121.

3. A Prayer of Thanksgiving: Psalms, chapter 107 or chapter 136. In the Standing Prayer emphasize, "and all the living will give thanks to You forever, selah."

4. Special prayers during holidays: It is worthwhile to pray for world peace. When saying such a prayer, one might add, "GOD of the World, give peace to the world, thereby allowing all living creatures that You created to enjoy all of Your

blessings." On the Sabbath one could recite from the book of Psalms, chapters 92 and 104.

5. Blessing before or after the meal: It is worthwhile that after the main meal of the day (whether at noon or in the evening) a Noahide should wash his hands if they have become soiled during the meal (before the meal there is no command for the Noahide to wash his hands in a ritual manner as do the Jews. This is specifically a Jewish practice. It is, however, necessary to wash them for sanitary purposes.) and utter a blessing of thanksgiving to GOD for the good that He has given to him. It can be something like this: "Blessed are You, King of the Universe, Who feeds the whole world with His goodness, pleasantness, grace and mercy. He gives bread to all flesh and the world is full of His mercy. Due to His great goodness, we have never lacked and will never be in need of food forever. His great Name feeds and gives everyone his livelihood, does good to everyone, and prepares food for all those that He has created." A person can, of course, change this, especially if some good things have occurred to him lately. Each person who chooses to say this prayer should do so individually (as opposed to having one

person say it for all). Clearly, these prayers are to be directed solely to GOD, and not to any intermediary.

6. Repentance: A Noahide who has sinned against GOD or his fellow man must repent and be sorry for what he has done. He must undertake that he will not commit this sin again. He should make a personal prayer to GOD, requesting mercy. If he has hurt a fellow person, or if he has done damage to that person's property, he must compensate him, as the people of Nineveh compensated each other, and he must request that person's forgiveness.

**Prohibition Against Influencing Others to Sin**

There is a prohibition against causing another person to err or commit sin as Pharaoh accused Abraham (Genesis 20:9) and the same concerning Avimelech who accused Isaac (Genesis 26:10).

In accordance with this, people should conduct themselves with modesty so as not to bring others to sin. In particular, women should apply this to their mode of dress and behavior.

## Holidays

### Sabbath

A Noahide should not observe the Shabbat in the manner that a Jew does. Nor should he make a point of abstaining from hard physical work on the Shabbat. A Noahide should not give occasion for a Jew to break the Shabbat.

There are those who say that every Ger Toshav (a non-Jew living in Eretz Yisrael in the time of the Jewish Temple, who has formally accepted the obligation to observe the Noahide laws in front of a Jewish court) has to uphold and keep the Sabbath (Rashi, Kritot 9, Yevamot 40). There is room to suggest that the Noahides, even nowadays, by accepting to fulfill the seven commandments, are in the same category as a Ger Toshav and should, according to Rashi, be required or at least allowed to keep the Shabbat.

So I (Rav Schwartz) would like to suggest that this is the way that the Noahides could celebrate the Seventh Day, a day of refraining from his vocation. On the eve of the Sabbath (Friday night), they might have a festive family dinner with special food and light candles after sundown in honor of the Seventh Day, which was given to Adam and Noah (and to make the Noahide celebration of the Shabbat distinct from the Jewish Shabbat observance). During the meal they may sing songs to strengthen their belief, including songs about the creation. They may read from the Torah. They should not call this day the Sabbath, but the Seventh Day as it is written in Genesis.

On the Seventh Day itself, if they can arrange it without difficulty, they should refrain from going to work. If possible, they should go out to the fields or a park so as to feel close to the Creator of the world. If the congregation holds a prayer session, they may recite the Psalms connected to the Sabbath and to the creation (like Psalm 104). Also they should study portions of the Torah connected to commandments of the children of Noah. They can study from the weekly portion of the Torah being read that Sabbath in the synagogues those subjects which concern all mankind and skipping those topics that concern specifically the Jews.

At the end of the Sabbath (Motzai Shabbat), the end of the Seventh Day and the beginning of the new week, they can recite the prayer for the new week (Havdalah) after having lit a havdalah candle, to thank GOD for having taught Adam how to make fire, which is the source of all energy that enabled man to make changes in this world. This Havdalah prayer, that separates the Seventh Day from the beginning of the week, can be recited as a Noahide wishes and can go something like this:

> Blessed are You our GOD, King of the Universe, Who differentiates between darkness and light, between day and night, between the Seventh Day

from the first day of the week, between the clean and the unclean, between the sacred and secular, between holy days and regular days, between Israel and the rest of the nations, who together are partners in one holy objective, to make Your Name holy in this world. AMEN.

**Rosh Hashanah**

Which is the first day of Tishrei is a day of reckoning for the whole world. The first day of Rosh Hashanah should be a day of repentance and deep inner thought about what a person has done during the past year. A Noahide should recite a prayer requesting that all the people of the world will accept and recognize the truth concerning the one true GOD. A Noahide can recite certain prayers from the Rosh Hashanah prayer book.

**Yom Kippur**

Yom Kippur is a day of repentance. While it is not a Noahide fast, repentance is a Noahide necessity.

**Succot (Feast of Tabernacles)**

It is stated in the book of Zechariah that after the Temple will be restored, during the holiday of Succoth all the nations of the world will make a pilgrimage to Jerusalem to bow down before GOD. Zechariah 14:1-21 states:

> And it shall come to pass that every one that is left of all the nations which come against Jerusalem shall even go up from year to year to worship the King, the Lord of hosts, and to keep the Feast of Tabernacles. And it shall be that whoever will not come up of all the families of the earth unto Jerusalem to worship the King, the Lord of hosts, even upon them shall be no rain. And if the family of Egypt go not up, and come not, that have no rain, there shall be the plague, which with which the Lord will smite the nations that come not up to keep this feast of Tabernacles. This shall be the punishment of Egypt, and the punishment of all nations that come not up to keep the feast of tabernacles. In that day shall there be upon the bells of the horses Holiness Unto the Lord; and the pots in the Lord's house shall be like the bowls before the altar. Yea every pot in Jerusalem and in Judah shall be holiness unto the Lord of hosts; and all they that sacrifice shall come and take of them and boil them; and in that day there shall be no more a Canaanite in the house of the Lord of hosts.

It is worthwhile for a person to take his vacation during this time. By doing so, a Noahide can use this free time to study, to observe nature and to meet with fellow Noahides for mutual prayer with emphasis on world peace just as Israelites did when the Temple existed and, as sacrifices were made for the welfare of all the nations, to pray for the coming of the Messiah who will amend the ways of the world.

**Hanukah**

Noahides are called to celebrate the victory of Judaism over Hellenism since this victory showed the world the strength of the Israelite's belief in the one true GOD, their true devotion and dedication in keeping the Torah and its commandments. It is also a time of special prayer for the restoration of the Tabernacle, the Temple and divine worship.

**Passover**

Passover is the first emancipation proclamation. It is advised that Noahides during this holiday should put a special stress on freedom for all humans. Although we do find slavery in the Torah, we must remember that the slavery mentioned there is a humane slavery. If one has a slave, then be a merciful master. Thoroughly cleaning ("spring cleaning") the house before this holiday would be a reminder of the slave labor of the Jews in Egypt. It also brings to mind the benefit that the exodus from Egypt brought to the world, a cleansing from the bad habits of mankind. On the eve of the first day of Passover, it is suggested that Noahides hold a festive meal with matzo and wine in honor of freedom.

**Shavuot**

Holiday commemorating the giving of the Torah. On this day there was a divine revelation and the human race acquired the Torah through it. It is a day that should be set aside for the study of Torah and the Noahide commandments.

# Commandments Dealing with Personal Matters

The purpose of the commandments is to correct the character traits of a person so that he can become closer GOD. Rabbi Abba Shaul in the Talmud explained a verse (Exodus 14, 2) as stating that we are to emulate those traits that GOD has revealed to us as being the principles that he uses in running the world. Rabbi Nissim Gaon in the preface to his commentary on the Talmud and Rabbi Moshe Feinstein in his responsa (Igrot Moshe, Yorah Deah vol. 2, chap. 130) wrote that all people are obligated to do all those things which are in the categories of ethics and proper character traits even though these actions are not specifically mentioned as being commanded.

Though the commandments have been divided into the two categories of between man and GOD and between man and his fellow, this distinction is an artificial one. This is because all commandments between a person and his fellow are also commandments between a person and GOD inasmuch as He has also commanded them.

## Concerning Food

The people of the nations are not limited in the food they are allowed to eat, except the eating of living flesh or the flesh and blood of a human being. There are also those authorities who are of the opinion that a Noahide should not eat the flesh of a dead animal unless killed for the specific purpose of eating its flesh.

These are the main points to the Jewish law (Halacha): This ritual law requires that the animal be slaughtered by severing the trachea and carotid artery in one stroke. This causes the least possible suffering to the animal. The animal must be totally dead, with all muscular and nerve flexing abated before one would be permitted to eat it. The lungs must be checked to determine that the animal was not afflicted with certain illnesses that would cause fatality according to the guidelines of the Jewish law.

## Animals for Eating

The people of other nations are allowed to eat all kinds of animals. Though there is a difference even for non-Jews between kosher and not kosher species, this is mainly regarding the sacrificial ritual and not for eating purposes.

[Why is it permitted for Noahides to eat any kind of animal whereas all animals were prohibited to Adam? It is written (Bereshit 9:3), "Every living thing that moves upon the earth shall be (as) food for you." Every living thing that moves includes cattle, beasts, birds, and even the fish of the sea. All of these are called "living things that move" (Ramban). Meat, which was prohibited to Adam, was permitted to Noah because (a) it was because of him and for his needs that GOD spared the animals; were it not for man they would not have been spared (cf. 6:7); (b) he toiled over them and attended to their needs in the ark. Of him it is said (Psalm 128:2): "You shall eat from the toil of your hands." He had thus acquired rights over them (Or HaChayim). "They were saved in an ark which you toiled to build; i.e. their salvation came through you; they are therefore yours to do with as you please like the green herbs of the field" (Bechor Shor; Chizkuni). "As the green herbage I have given you everything." Though I permitted only herbage, but not flesh, to Adam, I give you the same right to everything that he had for herbage" (Rashi). R' Bachya and Chizkuni comment that the comparison to green herbage is noteworthy: Lest one think that everything was permitted, God qualified His permission by comparing it to herbage. Just as some herbs are beneficial to man while others are unfit for food and even poisonous, so among the animals and birds there are those that are permitted by the Torah and those that are prohibited (see comm. of Chavel to his ed. of R' Bachya). This explains why, in spite of the general permission which was granted to Noah to consume meat, it is important that the Noahide not eat meat taken from a living animal, and the Jew eat only certain species slaughtered according to the Jewish law. Malbim explains that it is logical and desirable for a lower form of life to be eaten and absorbed into a higher form. Therefore, animals eat plant life, thus elevating it, and humans eat animals, elevating them to become part of intelligent man. (O that man would be intelligent!)]

**Flesh from the Living**

It is prohibited to eat meat that has been cut or torn off from a living creature, even from a dead animal, if the flesh was cut off when the animal was still alive or when it was on the verge of dying and not slaughtered according to Jewish law. If it was slaughtered by cutting its neck and not slaughtered by a Jew according to Jewish law, many of its' parts are considered to have been cut from a living animal and are therefore forbidden. This refers to all parts that are attached to the trachea and the esophagus and includes the lungs, liver, stomach, and intestines.

There are various methods used for killing the animals that are intended for human consumption. Some of them present no problem but others would call into question the permissibility of eating the above-mentioned organs. One should therefore either not eat those organs, verify that the method which was used to kill the animal was not by cutting its neck or, (and this is the most practical suggestion) only purchase the meat of such organs if it has been slaughtered by a Jew according to Jewish law, i.e. that is certified as kosher.

Nearly all the meat for human consumption today comes from animals that have been killed for eating. However some slaughterhouses detach parts of the body before the animal has stopped flexing its limbs. If a Noahide is not sure about the source of the meat, it is advised that he buy the meat from a person whom he can trust such as a fellow Noahide. In order to remove all doubt, it is possible to buy kosher meat with a kosher label from a recognized rabbinical organization. These rules of flesh from the living hold only toward animals and birds that have warm blood. It does not hold toward reptiles, creeping creatures and fish.

**Flesh from the Living is Mixed with Other Meat**

It is prohibited to eat meat that has been mixed with flesh from the living, whether it was done on purpose or not, even if cooked, broiled or added to a soup or any other type of drink.

**Naturalist**

The consumption of food should be mainly for health value. It is worthwhile though that a person should enjoy the food he eats since then the food is digested properly. There is also a spiritual value. If there is plenty of food on the table and it tastes good, a person feels and recognizes the grace of GOD. Food should be consumed to be healthy and not just for enjoyment. Therefore, a person must ensure his good health in everything that is connected with his diet. This includes a naturalist.

**Vegetarianism**

It is not good for a person to be a total vegetarian if he is doing so because he is trying to be merciful toward animals. There is a danger that such a person will feel that he has fulfilled his duty and will become unmerciful toward other species, including human beings. In his book, *Mein Kampf*, Hitler, the biggest criminal of the human race, said that he used to feed rats because he felt sorry for them. Of course, doctors have proven that it is not necessary to be excessive in the consumption of meat so as to remain healthy. Human teeth were created like those of an animal that eats vegetables and fruits. Adam was prohibited from eating meat. Only during the time of Noah was this prohibition lifted. This is because Noah saved animals from the flood and was allowed after that to eat meat. The Torah not only permits, but advises man to eat meat so that he recognizes the difference between man and animal. Rabbi Abraham Issac HaCohain Kook explained it in this way: "The Torah commanded us to eat meat for by doing so we realize that GOD gave us guidelines that teach us to be careful not to cause needless injury to other members of creation. If we are careful for these other members of creation, then we will be doubly sure of being careful in our daily contact with the crown of creation, which is mankind."

## Consumption of Alcoholic Beverages

A person should drink alcoholic beverages in moderation. To a Noahide it is enough to remind him of the sad story of Noah and the effects of his drunkenness after he planted a vineyard. A person who is an alcoholic should avoid use of alcohol.

## Keeping Healthy

A person should not indulge in things that are hazardous to his life and health. According to Genesis 9:5, a person is not allowed to commit suicide. From this we can learn that anything unhealthy is prohibited. This includes smoking, narcotics, alcohol abuse, and gluttony, exposing oneself to AIDS or other sexual diseases, driving when sleepy and taking unnecessary risks such as dangerous trips or pastimes. On the other hand a person can undertake dangerous professions, like building houses or picking fruits from tall trees because he is doing these things to build a better world and to find a livelihood for himself and his family.

## Ethical Behavior and Moral Values

1. A person should strive for better ethical and moral values. He should be merciful and should not harm animals unless it is for the benefit of humans, such as food, medical experiments and for work. Hunting just for sport and not to eat the animal's flesh or use its fur, is seen as cruelty to an animal and is inappropriate. A person must also be merciful and just toward his employees and servants. He is not

allowed to overwork or bring grief to his servants. According to the Rambam (Avadim 9:3), "A person must first feed his animals and servants before he sits to eat his own meal."

2. A person should strive not to be extreme in any character trait. For example, he should not be stingy; on the other hand, he should not overspend.

3. A person should strive to be humble. As Abraham said about himself, "and I am just dirt and ashes" (Genesis 18:2 7)

4. A person should strive to be truthful except in instances that the truth can bring harm to himself or others. An example is Abraham in the book of Genesis who said that his wife was his sister so that he would not be killed. In his defense, there was truth in his saying that she is his sister since his father was also her ancestor. Abraham was Sarah's uncle!

It is also permissible to change wording to preserve peace, but one must still be very careful about what he says. If the truth can bring harm, then it is not the truth. If the truth is harmful or shameful to the innocent, it should not be repeated. However, one should try not to lie to conceal the truth even for a good reason. He can simply refuse to comment or respond. Instead of saying, "I do not know" when you do know, say rather, "I cannot say," or "I have no comment." In explanation of this, the sages teach that when GOD wanted to create man, the angels were split on this issue. There were those who requested that GOD should not create man since mankind finds it difficult to say the truth, and their peace is full of disputes and fights. On the other hand, the angels that represented justice, grace, goodness, love, mercy, charity and benevolence called on GOD to create man. GOD threw truth to the ground, but not peace. From this the sages learned that truth that brings destruction and does not build is not truth. Thus a person is allowed to change his wording to bring peace.

5. A person must be grateful to whoever was kind and good to him. Joseph in his confrontation with Potiphar's wife (Genesis 39:9) explains his loyalty to a person that has been good to him which is reason enough not to sin, not to mention, that GOD also forbids it. Therefore a person must also honor his parents. One that disgraces his parents is liable to be punished.

6. Protecting the ecology is very important as long as it does not endanger human life.

7. A person should not be jealous. Cain killed Abel because of jealousy. In Pirkey Avot (4:20) it says that, "jealousy, lust and pursuit of honor remove a man from this world."

8. A person should be modest and chaste in his clothing. One of the sins that brought about the flood was that the people of that

time wore clothing that left inappropriate portions of the body exposed. He should be dressed appropriately for the occasion, be clean but not too conspicuous. According to Rashi, among the reasons that Jacob told his sons to go down to Egypt, (Genesis 42:1) was so that they would not be conspicuous in appearing as if the famine didn't concern them. From this we learn that a person should not be ostentatious, neither regarding himself nor his deeds.

9. A person should work even if he is financially well off. Agriculture is recommended since it brings him closer to GOD as he realizes that his welfare is dependent upon the rain that is in His hands. Today, agricultural work is not as it used to be, so if he tries to find another work he should look for something that will have a minimal danger of temptation and bring positive results.

10. A person should strive to be a peacemaker amongst the nations of the world and between fellow men. Rashi, in his commentary to Genesis 11:9, brings some sayings of the sages who explain why the generation of the tower of Babel, whose sins were worse than the sins of the generation of the flood, was punished less severely than the generation of the flood was punished. The reason is that there was love and peace among the generation of the tower. This goes to show to what high esteem GOD holds those who love peace.

## Arts

The arts help develop creativeness in a person, and this is positive and productive when used in the right way. This means that a person should be allowed to deal in the arts if it will encourage the development of good values and morality and not the opposite. For example, if a person deals in arts that are connected with pornography, he is dealing in negative matters. The same holds true in arts that encourage violence or harm to other human beings or laughter and ridicule of those persons who are less fortunate than others, not to speak of pseudo-scientific literature that speaks against the belief in the one true GOD and His Torah. On the other hand, if a person is gifted and uses this gift by producing beautiful things that bring honor to GOD, he is fulfilling GOD's wish.

## Pastime and Recreation

A person needs rest, but he should use this period of rest for the benefit of his physical and mental health. A person should not use his free time to engage in idle talk or matters that can bring him to sin. What a person does when he or she is away from home and among strangers decides that person's real character.

**Working For A Living**

1. Work as a moral value:

- GOD encouraged work to help mankind, as a moral value and in partnership in the work of the creations.

2. Restrictions in Agriculture

- It is recommended to not castrate men or animals because there was a great rabbi who was of the opinion that Noahides have taken upon themselves not to do this.
- It is forbidden to crossbreed animals and trees that are not of the same species. Breeding within a species in either the plant or animal kingdoms is permitted. It is permitted (even for Jews) to use and eat both animals and trees that were produced through forbidden crossbreeding.
- (Nowadays there are many things that can be done through genetic engineering. It may be that this is in the category of the prohibition of crossbreeding. One of the reasons given for the prohibition to crossbreed is that doing so implies disrespect for GOD's handiwork. It is as if one is declaring that those species that He created in His world are not enough.

- Though genetic engineering is not necessarily doing this, it may still imply a lack of respect for the Creator because it implies that the order of His creation is not good enough and is an attempt by man to improve on it. On the other hand there is no denying that man does have the right to try to improve a species and possibly genetic engineering is no different.)

3. A person should work as much as he can.

- This is true especially if he is a hired worker. This is true even if he is self-employed. We can learn this from Jacob who told the shepherds whom he met (Genesis 29:7), that they should not stop work at high noon.

4. Being a Faithful Worker

Jacob told his wives that he had worked with all his power under the employ of their father. A person should work in honesty and move away from dishonest ventures.

**Studying Science**

There is value in studying science, especially since this enables a person to recognize the greatness of GOD and to better the creation for the benefit of society. All this is under the condition that it be done in a proper manner and not by unbelievers who want to liberate themselves or take over the world from GOD, which was the first sin made by a man.

1. Healing with the aid of Doctors and Medicines

- As it is stated in Exodus that a doctor should heal, our sages learned that a person who can heal his fellow human being should do so, that a sick person must go to a doctor to be healed. The important point here is that he should not rely on doctors alone, but in GOD who is the true doctor. The person should make an effort to get well.

2. Transplanting of Organs

- This is allowed to save the life of a person as long as the life of another person is not shortened so as to withdraw organs from him.

3. Unnecessary Dangers

- A person should be careful about medical treatment and medicines so as not to fall into unnecessary dangers like a dangerous plastic surgery that can have serious effects on the health of a person. If the dangerous surgery or treatment is being carried out to try to save the person's life, then it is allowed.

## 4. The Purposes of Medical Treatments

- The main purpose is to increase the life span of a person and to prevent suffering, to increase fertility, but not to increase the pleasure of a person. It is prohibited to cause abortion without the medical reason of saving the life of the pregnant woman. (As it is not certain that a Noahide is permitted to perform an abortion even in such a situation, one should try to find a Jewish doctor to do it.)
- A doctor is not allowed to stop the suffering of his patient by shortening his life.

## 5. Medical Experiments

- If such experiments endanger the life of the patient, but there is a chance that it can save his life, it is allowed. However, there is a need for the approval of the patient. It is not enough to request the permission of the family. It also may be allowed if the experiment might help a terminal patient who otherwise will die. A rabbi who is an expert in Jewish law should be consulted before doing such a thing.
- If the experiment cannot endanger the patient, it is worthwhile to receive the patient's approval because

there might be some side effects, or it might endanger him later.

## Patriotism

A person should be faithful to his country and leader. A person should not only pray for the welfare of his country but for all the world and humanity. It is forbidden to evade paying taxes and customs. Tax evasion is not to be confused with tax avoidance. Tax evasion is criminal. However, one is allowed to avoid paying taxes by using all possible deductions, depreciation, amortization and transfers of properties to heirs before death to avoid taxation. It is legal and should be pursued.

## Vows, Oaths and Pledges

A pledge is a positive mild commitment, "If I can, I will." It is a matter of conscience and ability to fulfill. It is probably appropriate that it should be fulfilled.

A vow is a commitment made to someone else. It should be fulfilled because of the obligation to abide by the laws of interpersonal relationships.

An oath is an unconditional commitment. When undertaken in the name of GOD it must be honored because of one's duty to respect GOD. Abraham made Eliezer place his hand under his thigh and swear by an oath (Genesis 23:2-3). A person must keep all vows, and oaths he made, especially if he has promised to give alms to the needy or a sacrifice to GOD.

## Commandments Dealing with Matters Between Man and His Fellow

**The Prohibition Against Murder**

Every man must safeguard the most important deposit given in the custody of humanity, the lives of human beings, be it his own life or that of others. It is therefore prohibited for a person to endanger himself and, even more so, others. He should be careful to guard his own health and that of society and not do those things that are likely to cause harm like driving with excessive speed, etc.

A person is prohibited from murdering any person, adult or child, man or woman and even the fetus in a womb. However, abortion is allowed if it will save the life of the mother.

It is prohibited to kill a sick person although he is dying of a terminal disease, and there is no possibility of saving his life and even if the patient himself requests to die. Taking organs from such a person while he is still alive, although it may save another person's life, is also prohibited. If it is known that there is no chance of saving life, there is no need to prolong suffering by artificial means since the patient is dying anyway. However, we are not allowed to directly disconnect the equipment that allows the dying person to breathe.

It is forbidden to kill a criminal before he is brought to trial and sentenced by a court. A person is not allowed to commit suicide or to shorten his own life in any way. If he is being forced to commit idol worship, he is allowed to commit suicide to sanctify the name of GOD. If a person is being forced to kill another person or be killed, he is still not allowed to kill others. However, if the killers are demanding that one person be handed over to them or they will kill everyone, it is allowed to hand over that one person to save the lives of all the others. However, in the case of terrorists, it should be considered that such demands by terrorists have only proven to encourage the killers to take more hostages and kill more people.

If a person is running after you or chasing you to do you harm but not to kill you, then you are not allowed to kill him. However, if his purpose is to kill, and you have no other way in which to save your life but to kill him, you are allowed to do so in self-defense. But if there is any other way that you can save your life, perhaps by injuring him just enough to stop him from chasing you, then you are not allowed to kill him. If you do slay the murderer, you are guiltless and may save other people's lives who the murderer might otherwise kill later. Thus if the killing is to save your life or someone else's life, you are allowed to kill him. It is even a mitzvah to do so as Abraham went out to war to save Lot, his nephew and others. Here Abraham was saving life, not killing one who is trying to kill him.

It is prohibited to declare war on another nation since you will be involved in killing and you are endangering the lives of your people too. You are allowed to go out to war if you are being attacked. You are allowed to kill the attackers, but you are not allowed to kill prisoners of war if they are no longer endangering life.

## Prohibition Against Spoil, Plunder, and Harming the Rights of Others

### Embarrassing

A person is not allowed to insult or injure the reputation of another person in public. It is better that he be thrown into a burning fire rather than to embarrass someone else. An example is Tamar who avoided publicly shaming Judah even though she had been sentenced to be burnt. Tamar was a child of Noah.

### Hitting another person

It is prohibited to hit another person or to injure him. Parents or teachers are allowed to hit their children to discipline them and in self-protection. You are also permitted to fight back if you are attacked.

### Property, goods and possessions of others

It is prohibited to cause damage to such things. If a person is given such a possession to safeguard or for any other reason even if it is worthless, it must be returned to its legal owner. You cannot keep it. A person is also not allowed to cheat on taxes.

## Returning lost property

When a country has laws concerning the return of lost property, then such goods must be handed over to the rightful owner.

## Prohibition against cheating in business and weights

A person is not only prohibited from doing so, but he must make every effort to protect his credibility by carrying out his business transactions in the most honest and honorable way possible.

## Coveting other person's property

This means property, money or anything belonging to another. It is prohibited to covet belongings of another, which means to scheme to acquire them by illegal methods against the will of the present owner. It is forbidden to sue for damages against any individual, company or government when there was no real damage done or for an exorbitant proportion.

## Bribery

It is prohibited to give or accept bribes. Sometimes one may find himself in circumstances that cause him to pay a bribe, but this would be in a place where there is no justice, such as among robbers or the like, so as to save oneself.

## Grace, Mercy, Charity, Kindness and Benevolence

A Noahide is called upon to give to charities and persons in need. According to Rav Saadiah Gaon, it is commendable for a person to tithe, meaning that he set aside up to one tenth of all his earnings for this purpose. However, a person need not deprive himself of his own basic necessities in order to give to others. According to Ezekiel, one of the reasons for the punishment of Sodom was that the poor people there were not given alms. It is worthwhile that a person keep a special account for such a purpose, and once a week or month he should transfer it to good causes. It is best to transfer it directly to the needy people.

A Noahide is called upon to act in a graceful manner and to be benevolent. One should be hospitable and a good host with all his heart as Abraham did.

## Eight Degrees of Charity

There are eight degrees of charity, one higher than the other:

1. The highest degree is to aid a man who is in danger of losing his financial independence by offering him a gift or a loan, by entering into partnership with him, or by providing work for him, so that he may remain self supporting.

2. The next highest degree is where the one who gives and the one who receives are not aware of the identity of each other.

3. The third, inferior degree is when the giver knows who the recipient is, but the recipient does not know who the giver is.

4. The fourth, still lower degree is where the recipient knows who the giver is, but the giver does not know who the recipient is.

5. The fifth degree is where the giver puts the alms into the hands of the poor without being asked.

6. The sixth degree is where he puts the money into the hands of the poor after being asked.

7. The seventh degree is where he gives less than he should but does so cheerfully.

8. The eighth degree is where he gives resentfully.

**Courts of Justice**

It is important to form courts of justice so that persons can be called upon to uphold the mitzvot, the religious laws and to be able to judge between people. Sages were divided as to whether the Noahides should be judged according to the Torah concerning financial matters or whether they should be judged according to common sense. It is worthwhile that such courts of justice should give sentences according to the same law for men and for women. The judges should be men since a woman should strive not to be involved in public matters.

Every person should go to a court for justice and not try to mete out justice himself. Courts of justice are allowed to enforce regulations for the benefit of the society and to improve ethics and morality. It is the obligation of the Noahide to execute justice to the fullest degree and not to be merciful to criminals. People have the obligation to obey the law and see that the legislative and judicial and personnel and systems obey the law.

**Marriage and Sex**

Every man should marry a woman, and every woman should marry a man since it is written "that it is not good for a man to live alone by himself." Marriage brings about a partnership between two people and increases the population of the world. In marriage a Noahide will participate and contribute in the building of the world.

Marriage is initiated by the couple's decision to live together as husband and wife followed by their sexual union. It is worthwhile and enhancing that the two hold a formal marriage ceremony and a marriage feast.

A married couple can divorce even if both don't agree to the divorce. If the husband sends his wife away from their home declaring that they are no longer married or if the wife leaves their home with a similar declaration they are no longer married. However, Noahides should abide by the laws of the state in which they live in marriage matters. They should therefore also follow any procedures that are required by the laws where they live so that they should be considered divorced also according to these laws. After the divorce, both partners are free to remarry. The marriage also ends if one of the two dies.

According to the Torah, a married woman and another man are not allowed to have sexual or any intimate relations with each other. A man, on the other hand, is allowed to marry more than one wife or concubine. Since the 10th century the Ashkenazic Jews generally have only one wife. Today there are also civil laws in many countries against bigamy, which are to be followed as law for the Noahide. A person is not allowed to have sexual relations with his mother, sisters, maternal aunts from his father or mother's side, his father's wife even after the death of his father, daughter, granddaughter, daughter-in-law, mother-in-law and her mother, his wife's daughters and granddaughters. A person is not allowed to have homosexual relations (man with another man or a woman with another woman). Also a person is not allowed to have sexual relations with animals. This is beastiality.

Rape by a Noahide is a capital offence. There are opinions that, regarding people who are forbidden by the Torah to have sex with one another, the Torah prohibits any physical contact between them that is liable to be stimulating. This would include kissing, hugging and social dancing. It is nevertheless permitted for people to kiss their offspring.

It is worthwhile for men and women to minimize their mingling with one another. For this reason, youth groups and social activities should be organized separately for boys and for girls. In particular, when groups come together for prayer, etc. the men and the women should sit separately.

The purpose of sexual relations is to increase the human race and to strengthen the ties between the married couple. According to the Torah, a husband is called to gratify and satisfy sexually his wife. The same holds true for the wife toward her husband. All this is to strengthen the ties between the married couple. GOD created men and women with sexual appetite and chemistry. Sex is a blessing from GOD, and it is not sin in the bounds of permitted sex under the seven laws of Noah.

One should not read pornographic literature or watch pornographic movies. As women who are dressed inappropriately can stimulate men easily, women should dress modestly.

Most authorities are of the opinion that Bnei Noah are not obligated any more to have children. There is a minority view that they are. According to this minority view and the view of Nachmanides, masturbation is prohibited. Also, according to them only the female is allowed to use contraceptives. The ones that would be permitted are foam or pills or similar methods.

It is an ancient custom of Israel to be careful and not to have sexual relations when the woman is having her menstrual period. An Israelite married woman is not allowed to have sexual relations with her husband for seven days, starting from the first day of her menstruation period. After the seven days she must go to a ritual bath, a mikvah, before she resumes having sexual relations with her husband. A Noahide is not called to do so, but it is worthwhile for the couple to abstain from having sexual relations during the woman's menstrual period.

*Personal Notes*

## Noahide Commandments

*Service From the Heart*

## Noahide Commandments

## Service From the Heart

# About Disposal of this Siddur

By
Rabbi Yechiel Sitzman

---

Regarding the eventual disposal of the Siddur, these were produced by machine and have no intrinsic holiness; it is the text which is holy, but not the object per se.

These may be disposed of (in the garbage) as long as the nature of the object is not visible in the process. Thus, wrapping in a (biodegradable) plastic bag that is not transparent is sufficient. For "safety" it is recommended that one bag be wrapped inside another.

The main point of this is to prevent dishonor to the texts.

*A belief that does not bring in its wake a fulfillment and a change, is a false one.*

*Soren Kirkgegard*

# *Glossary*

**Av** – The darkest events in Jewish history (the destruction of both Temples) occurred during the first week and a half of this month, particularly The Nine Days which culminate in Tisha B'Av. However, there is a minor and largely unknown holiday during the full moon of the month called Tu B'Av which was, in ancient times, one of the happiest days of the year.

**Avadim** - slaves

**Avot** - "Fathers" or "Patriarchs" It can also be translated as "Elders" or "Sages".

**Bavli** – *Talmud Bavli* (Babylonian Talmud)

**B'deken** - The veiling of the bride by the groom. This custom developed from the biblical story of Jacob, who married Leah by mistake, instead of Rachel, the woman he loved.

**Beersheva** - Beer means well, sheva means seven or oath – thus Beersheva means the Seven Wells or the Well of the Oath.

**Berechos** – A Tractate of the Talmud

**Bereshit – Genesis**

**Bnei No'ach or B'nai Noah** – *Lit.* Children of Noah; refers to non-Jews who strive to live by the basic laws for humanity derived from the Torah

**Children of Noah** – descendants of Noah commonly referred to as Noahide.

**Covenant** - Various contracts between God and Mankind

**Emunah** – Faith

**Eretz Yisrael** – The land of Israel

**Gedaliah** – refers to **The Fast of Gedalia** (or **Gedaliah**) is a Jewish fast day from dawn till dusk to lament the assassination of the righteous governor of Judah of that name, which left Judah devoid of any Jews and Jewish rule, and made the destruction of the first Temple complete.

**Gemara** – Discussions of the Rabbis in the Talmud, Also used as a synonym the Talmud.

**Genesis Rabbah** - (**Bereshit Rabba**) It is a midrash comprising a collection of ancient rabbinical homiletical interpretations of the book of Genesis (*Bereshit* in Hebrew).

**Ger Toshav** - Gentile resident in Israel who makes a commitment before a Jewish Court to live by the Seven Laws of Noahide (No official recognition until the Temple is restored)

**Gentile** - non-Jew.

**Halacha** – "The Way" Hebrew for Law

**Hashem** - Hebrew for "the Name" some say "Adonai" (Lord) when it is read for liturgical purposes, also found in Leviticus 24:11

**Havdalah** - The prayer for the end of the Seventh day and the beginning of the new week.

**Kashrut** – Kosher, concerning the permissibility of food to be consumed by a Jew.

**Kritot** 9 – Tractate and page within the tractate of the Talmud

**Kuzari** – written by R. Yehudah HaLevi and was based on the historical event of the conversion to Judaism of King Bulan and the majority of his people, the Khazars.

**Maharal from Prague** - Rabbi Judah Loew (1525-1609)

**Malbim** – Rabbi Meir Leibush (1809-1879) Commentator of the Tanach

**Matriarch -** A highly respected woman who is a mother.

**Matzo** – unleavened bread

**Melachim** – The Book of Kings

**Mesilat Yesharim** – "Path of the Just" by HaRav Moshe Chaim Luzzato

**Midrash -** From the Hebrew *darash*, "to inquire," Refers to the "commentary" literature developed in classical Judaism that attempts to interpret Jewish Scriptures in a thorough manner.

**Mishna** – Ancient Oral Teachings of the Torah Laws

**Mitzvot-** commandments of the Torah

**Motzai Shabbat** – Hebrew for Saturday night

**Nineveh** – See the book of Jonah in your Bible

**Noahide or Noachide** – Non-Jew who accepts and lives by the Torah as it applies to him/her.

**Or HaChayim -** classic Torah commentary of Rabbi Chayim ben Attar

**Pagan** – Idolater

*Glossary*

**Passover** – Holyday commemorating the Exodus from Egypt.

**Patriarch** – The father and ruler of a family or tribe.

**Pirkey Avot - Sayings of the Father's,** Tractate of the Talmud that consists of six chapters. It begins with an order of transmission of the tradition from Moses receiving the Torah at Sinai who then transmits it, through various generations, eventually to the Rabbis (Avot 1:1).

**Polytheistic** – refers to one who believes in or worships multiple gods

**Polytheism** – Belief in or the worship of multiple gods

**Prayer Garment** – A garment that some choose to wear with a rainbow theme incorporated into the making of it so they are not confused to be Jewish, most without TzitTzit (fringe on the four corners) and if they are used they must be tied in a different manner than Israel's, Can be worn during morning prayers or communal prayer.

**Rabbi Yehudah HaLevi** –A great Torah Scholar who lived from 1075 C.E. – 1141 C.E.

**Rambam** – (1135-1204) Moses ben Maimon (Maimonides) perhaps one of the greatest thinkers in all of Jewish history, Maimonides was a physician, commentator and philosopher. Who was best known for his Guide for the Perplexed, and his Mishneh Torah, an "easy-to-use"

compilation of Jewish law **Rav** - Hebrew word for Rabbi

**Rav Hasdai** – Talmudic Scholar

**Rav Saadiah Gaon**- Philosopher, translator, and Talmudist.

**Rashi** – Acronym for Rabbi Shlomo Yitzhaqi; Acclaimed for his ability to present the basic meaning of the text in a concise yet lucid fashion, Rashi appeals to both learned scholars and beginning students, and his works remain a centerpiece of contemporary Jewish study.

**Righteousness** - characterized by uprightness or morality; morally right or justifiable; acting in an upright, moral way; virtuous.

**Rosh Hashanah** - The Jewish New Year commemorating the creation of the universe; universal Day of Judgment.

**Sage** – Some one who is wise, perceptive and discerning.

**Shem** - One of Noah's sons, Also (Melchizedek) King of righteousness or Righteous King, was the King of Salem (Jerusalem)

**Shema** – (Hebrew for hear or listen) Declaration from Deut.6:4

**Shofar** – Horn made from a Ram's horn.

**Scholar** – A learned person, one trained in a special branch of learning or an advanced student.

**Sefer** - Book

# Glossary

**Sefer Ha'Chinuch** – Book of Education

**Selah** – Notation used in Psalms (Songs) to indicate a musical pause.

**Shabbat** – The Seventh Day

**Shabbat 88a** – Tractate and page within the tractate of the Talmud.

**Siddur** –"order" refers to the orderly manner in which prayers are laid out.

**Sifri Vetchanan** - Oldest rabbinic commentary on Deut. 3:23-7:11

**Sota** – Tractate of the Talmud`

**Sukkot** - Celebration of Sukkot is done in recognition of the temporary dwellings built by the Israelites and the mixed multitude (non-Jews) who journeyed from Egypt to Kenaan (Canaan); Also, the sixth tractate in the Mishnah order of Moed (appointed times), dealing with laws related to the festival of Sukkot.

**Ta'anit** – Tractate of the Talmud

**Talmud** - From the Hebrew word "lamed"--to study; an encyclopedic collection of legal interpretations based upon the Mishnah.

**Tammuz** - A month of the Hebrew calendar

**Tanya** – An Chassidic work by Rebbe Shneur Zalman of Liadi.

**Tanna (Tannaim)** – Rabbis of the period of the Mishnah

**Tanna d'bei Eliyahu** - The name of an ancient Midrash

**Temple Mount** – Mount Moriah, the place where Adam, Able, Noah, Abraham, Isaac, Jacob built alters and offered sacrifices, also where the Holy Temple was built.

**The Gaon, Rabbi Shmuel Ben Hafni** – An especially learned Torah Scholar.

**Tevet** – A month of the Hebrew calendar.

**Tiferet Yisrael** – A well-known commentary on the Mishna by Israel Lipschitz of Danzig (1782-1860)

**Tishrei** - Hebrew Month

**Torah** - The first five books of the Hebrew Bible; also used in a more general sense to include all Jewish religious literature.

**Tzadikim** – (plural of Tzadik, Heb., and "righteous one") A Hebrew term for a righteous person, or a spiritual leader.

**Yevamot** 40 – Tractate and page within the tractate of the Talmud

**Yomah** 28b – Tractate and page within the tractate of the Talmud

**Zion** - a term that most often designates the land of Israel and its capital Jerusalem. The word is found in texts dating back almost three millennia. It originally referred to a specific mountain near Jerusalem (Mount Zion)

**Zohar** – Hebrew/Aramaic Rabbinical, Kabbalistic work that is one of the most influential with Chassidim.

*Personal Notes*

*Service From the Heart*

# More Information

The approbation for this book does not extend to Internet sources or any other book. Because the Internet is constantly changing, sources may not always be available or suitable. Always consult an orthodox rabbi about the appropriateness of Internet sources.

| Online Education | |
|---|---|
| http://messiahtruth.com | http://www.virtualyeshiva.com |
| http://www.aish.com | http://www.okbns.org |
| http://lazerbrody.typepad.com | http://www.geocities.com/rachav7 |

| Books | Author or Publisher |
|---|---|
| **Torah Study** | |
| The Stone Edition Chumash | Artscroll Mesorah |
| The Pentateuch And Haftorahs | Hertz/Soncino |
| The Guide for the Perplexed | Maimonides |
| Interlinear Pirkei Avos. | Schottenstein Edition |
| **Seven Laws of Noah Studies** | |
| A Light Unto the Nations | Rabbi Yoel Schwartz |
| The Seven Laws of Noah | Aaron Lichtenstein |
| Path of the Righteous Gentile | Clorfene and Rogalsky |
| Seven Colors of the Rainbow | Reb Yirmeyahu Bindman |
| Mishnah Torah, Laws of Kings | Maimonides |

Contemporary Halakhic Problems V. II    J. David Bleich

**Further Reading**

The Noahide Code                 Alan W. Cecil

Israel and Humanity               Benamozegh

The Way of God                    Torah Classics

**For Children**

The Colorful Rainbow Dream      Daphne Cohen

*Personal Notes*

## Service From the Heart

# More Information

For more publications and free downloads from OKBNS PRESS please visit our website at http://www.okbns.org.

www.ingramcontent.com/pod-product-compliance
Lightning Source LLC
Chambersburg PA
CBHW031308150426
43191CB00005B/121